A Question of Freedom

A Question of Freedom

A Memoir of Learning,

Survival,

and Coming of Age

in Prison

———

R. Dwayne Betts

AVERY

a member of Penguin Group (USA) Inc.

New York

Published by the Penguin Group

Penguin Group (USA) Inc., 375 Hudson Street, New York, New York 10014, USA • Penguin Group (Canada),
90 Eglinton Avenue East, Suite 700, Toronto, Ontario M4P 2Y3, Canada (a division of Pearson Penguin Canada Inc.) •
Penguin Books Ltd, 80 Strand, London WC2R 0RL, England • Penguin Ireland, 25 St Stephen's Green, Dublin 2, Ireland
(a division of Penguin Books Ltd) • Penguin Group (Australia), 250 Camberwell Road, Camberwell, Victoria 3124, Australia
(a division of Pearson Australia Group Pty Ltd) • Penguin Books India Pvt Ltd, 11 Community Centre, Panchsheel Park,
New Delhi–110 017, India ▪ Penguin Group (NZ), 67 Apollo Drive, Rosedale, North Shore 0632, New Zealand
(a division of Pearson New Zealand Ltd) • Penguin Books (South Africa) (Pty) Ltd, 24 Sturdee Avenue,
Rosebank, Johannesburg 2196, South Africa

Penguin Books Ltd, Registered Offices: 80 Strand, London WC2R 0RL, England

First trade paperback edition 2010
Copyright © 2009 by R. Dwayne Betts

"Shahid Reads His Own Palm" from *Shahid Reads His Own Palm.* Copyright © 2010 by Reginald Dwayne Betts.
Reprinted with the permission of Alice James Books. "Shahid Reads His Own Palm" first appeared in
the *Crab Orchard Review.*

"The Bees." Copyright © 1974 by Audre Lorde, from The Collected Poems of Audre Lorde by Audre Lorde.
Used by permission of W.W. Norton & Company, Inc.

Excerpt from "For Freckle-Faced Gerald" from *The Essential Etheridge Knight*, by Etheridge Knight, © 1986.
Reprinted by permission of the University of Pittsburgh Press.

Most Avery books are available at special quantity discounts for bulk purchase for sales
promotions, premiums, fund-raising, and educational needs. Special books or book
excerpts also can be created to fit specific needs. For details, write Penguin Group (USA) Inc.
Special Markets, 375 Hudson Street, New York, NY 10014.

The Library of Congress catalogued the hardcover edition as follows:

Betts, R. Dwayne.
A question of freedom : a memoir of learning, survival, and coming of age in prison / R. Dwayne Betts.
p.   cm.
ISBN 978-1-58333-348-8
1. Betts, R. Dwayne. 2. Prisoners—Virginia—Biography. 3. Prisons—Virginia. I. Title.
HV9468.B48A3   2009   2009021837
365'.42092—dc22
[B]

ISBN 978-1-58333-396-9 (paperback edition)

Printed in the United States of America
9 10 8

BOOK DESIGN BY MICHELLE McMILLIAN

*Penguin is committed to publishing works of quality and integrity. In that spirit,
we are proud to offer this book to our readers; however, the story,
the experiences, and the words are the author's alone.*

For my wife.
Terese Marie, I couldn't have written a word without you.

For my son—every day my life means more because of you.

And for Moms, who forgave me and believed
even when I'd soaked our life in tears.

Contents

Part I. The New World

Shahid Reads His Own Palm

I come from the dusty hands of men who used
    the smoldering end of blunts to blow shotguns,
men who arranged their lives around the mystery
    of the moon breaking a street corner in half;
past the sweat in my empty palms and the praying
    woman knelt before Planned Parenthood. I come
from "Swann Road" written in a child's huge
    and slanted block letters across a playground fence,
the orange globe with black stripes in Bishop's left
    hand, untethered and rolling to the sideline,
a crowd open-mouthed, waiting to see the end
    of the sweetest crossover in a Virginia state prison.
I come from Friday night's humid and musty air,
    Junk Yard Band cranking heavy in a stolen Bonneville,
a tilted bottle of Wild Irish Rose against my lips,
    and King Hedley's secret written in the lines of my palm.
I come from beneath a cloud of white smoke, a lit pipe
    and the way glass heats rocks into a piece of heaven.
A bullet in an unfired snub nosed revolver, tofu scrambled
    with garlic and purple onion, and every day
the small muscles in my finger threaten to pull
    a trigger, slight and curved like my woman's eyelashes.

A Question of Freedom

———

The New World

This hour I tell things in confidence,
I may not tell everybody but I will tell you.

—Walt Whitman, "Song of Myself"

Thirty Minutes

Sixteen years hadn't even done a good job on my voice. It cracked in my head as I tried to explain away the police car driving my one hundred and twenty-six pounds to the Fairfax County Jail. Everything near enough for me to touch gleamed with the color of violence: the black of the deputy's holstered guns, the broken leather of the seat I sat on and the silver of the cuffs that held my hands before me in prayer. When I closed my eyes I thought about the way the gun felt in my palm. I tried to remember what caliber pistol it was, but couldn't. It was automatic and weighed nothing in my palm, and I couldn't figure how something that weighed nothing could have me slumped in the back of a car driving me away from my life. My wrists almost slipped through cuffs that held me captive as jailhouse dangers swirled red in my head.

I want to tell you that I could talk tough, that I was going over every way I knew to say fuck you. But I wasn't. There were titles of movies and books on my mind: *Shawshank Redemption; American Me; Blood In, Blood Out; Makes Me Wanna Holler; Racehoss; The*

Autobiography of Malcolm X. Every movie or book I'd ever read about prison bled with violence and I knew the list I was making in my head could go on forever. Stories of robbery, rape, murder, discrimination and what it means to not be able to go home. Sixteen years old and I was headed to a jail cell, adding my name to the toll of black men behind bars. Not even old enough to buy liquor or cigarettes, but I knew I'd be stepping into the county jail in minutes and that my moms was at home somewhere crying.

When I tried to part my hands I thought about the violence, about how real it is when a cell door closes behind you at night. I thought about needing a knife, 'cause from what I knew everyone needed a knife. I stared at my shackled feet. I hadn't seen my Timberlands since the day I was arrested, three months earlier.

I was getting ready to learn what it meant to lock your thoughts inside of yourself and survive in a place governed by violence, a place where violence was a cloud of smoke you learned to breathe in or choked on. Sometimes there's a story that's been written again and again, sometimes a person finds himself with a story he thinks will be in vogue forever. The story is about redemption, about overcoming. A person finds that story and starts to write it, thinking it will do him some good to tell the world how it really was. That's not this story. This is about silence, and how in an eight-year period I met over a dozen people named Juvenile or Youngin or Shorty, all nicknames to tell the world that they were in prison as young boys, as children. We wore the names like badges of honor, because in a way, for some of us, it was all we had to guard us against the fear. And we were guilty and I was just like everyone else: I thought about the edge of a knife.

My world before incarceration was black and white. Suitland, Maryland, the closest thing to the black belt that I'd ever seen. And it wasn't just that there were no white people in my community, it was that as a kid we always saw the white people around us as intruders or people looking to have power. Teachers, firefighters, cops or the white folks we saw on buses and trains who we imagined driving into D.C. from their nice neighborhoods to work. One night at a mall in Springfield, Virginia, changed my world. It only took thirty minutes. Brandon and I walked into a mall that literally had more white people in it than I'd ever seen at one time. And we had walked in looking for someone to make a victim. Both of us were in high school. We should have been thinking homework, basketball and pretty girls. Driving to the jail brought the night in Springfield fresh to my memory. Somewhere between pulling out a pistol that fit nicely in the palm of my hand, tapping lightly on the window of a forest green Grand Prix and waking the sleeping middle-aged white man with the muzzle of the burner, I committed six felonies. It was February of 1996 and I was a high school junior. I'd never held a gun before and was an honor student who could almost remember every time the police had spoken to me, but I knew none of that mattered as my face pressed against the window of the cruiser.

I wore a sweater of swirling greens and oranges woven and layered as collage; a cheap imitation Gucci that I had buried long ago in my closet. I remember when my moms bought it. I begged for the sweater, thinking if it fooled me it would fool my friends. I was dead wrong. The first time I wore it to school six people joned on me, cut me up so bad that I dumped it under a rack of old clothes and books. It happened a year before I got locked up, when I was in tenth grade and impressing the finest girl in my chemistry class ruled every other ambition. The sweater resurfaced when I needed court clothes. My mother told me that I needed something nice to wear to court. The judges were always white. There may have been black judges but I never saw or stood before one the entire time I trekked back and forth to court. The juvenile judge who watched me stand uncomfortable in the sweater I ended up wearing to the jail didn't care how I looked. He stared at the charges before me and agreed with the prosecutor to pass me over to adult court before I could speak. It was all policy, a formality that my lawyer knew about. He told me, "Don't worry. This was a formality I knew was coming. The law says that certain charges are automatically certifiable, and carjacking is one of them, but in Circuit Court the judge will have more discretion."

What he was really saying was that nothing I wore mattered. Clothes could hide me no more than days of smoking weed made people think I was built for running the streets. The law said the gun, the carjacking, the robbery all made it an argument we couldn't win. Three things that meant my past didn't matter and certification as an adult was automatic. It's like the car, the cuffs, the shackles and even the drive were as good as guaranteed when I pulled a pistol on that sleeping white man.

All I had with me was my body and a black trash bag that an officer took from me as they led me to a bench in a corner. On my lips and in my head was the start of a new language defined by the way words changed meanings, all because I'd decided to make a man a victim. New words like *inmate, state number* and *juvenile certification* had crept into my vocabulary. An *inmate* is what I'd become as soon as the deputies picked me up from the juvenile detention center. It meant I was in the custody of the Fairfax County Jail, and the most important thing anyone needed to know about me was my *state number.* It was a five-digit number I soon learned meant more than my name. It said I was who I said I was whenever I walked around the jail with the band they attached to my arm.

At Landmark we weren't inmates, we were juvenile offenders, which was a nice way of saying black boy in jail from what I saw, because that's all we were at Landmark. Landmark Detention Center was a juvenile facility that housed boys and girls. Mostly the kids were in there for fighting or truancy or selling drugs. There was one white boy in there with us; everyone else was black. Four small units that were as secure as any prison. Everything was electronic and you could only move when told to. But you got to go to school, had to go to school, and the uniform was sweatpants and a T-shirt. That meant if you tried hard enough you could have imagined yourself at an extended camp. Unless of course you were me, given a single cell in the corner and a note on your door that said no roommate because you were waiting to be transferred to the jail.

It didn't take long for me to move from inside the squad car to inside the jail. Voices jumped around me in a chaos that belongs to jails and prisons. The same officers who'd driven me to the jail were with me. "You know this jail isn't like the place we're taking you from. All you kids in there running around trying to be tough. Well, you're going where they say the tough guys are." The officer wanted to scare me. He was standing as I sat, looking down and probably imagining a scene from the nightly news of a gun-toting young black man gone crazy. He probably thought about the victim and what they say on TV about black boys who pull guns on people. Fear was a commodity everyone traded in. In three months I'd learned that everyone from lawyers to the judges to the other kids around me thought their power rested in getting someone to fear you. After the arrest warrant had been signed there was only fear and violence. But there had been fear and violence in my life before. Fights in the streets when my arms stopped working after taking too many jabs, or afternoons I spent running from fights. It all caught up with me when I started believing that fear and violence were the things power was made of, and I wanted to touch it if only for a moment.

Thirty minutes changed my life. It took less than thirty minutes for me to find the sleeping man in his car, and it took less than thirty minutes for me to get to the jail. When I walked in, the rank smell of the place hit my nostrils like the fat end of a bat. It made me feel like a man who'd spent a week sleeping in his own piss and shit, breathing it until shit was the only important thing left in the world. Outside the sun lit up the sky but in there it was past dark. A toothless man in the holding cell across from where I stood drooled and yelled at the bars before him. I was embarrassed. It had taken thirty minutes for me to commit the crime that made me a statistic. *Statistic*—another word that took on new meaning after I found my hands in cuffs. I was on a bench in the basement of the Fairfax County Jail waiting for an officer to tell me what cell I'd be spending the night in. I was a *statistic*, another word for failure, and it hurt because no matter what the prosecutors thought, I not only didn't want to be in jail, I really didn't want to be the person pulling guns on people. The jail's smell was funky, but since people were used to the smell eyes kept drifting to me, the young boy sitting on the bench in the corner. The smell was somebody's breath after they've thrown up a plastic cup of Hennessy; piss saturated into someone's clothes, into their skin; but not as noticeable to them as my shaking hands and fresh face.

"Good luck, kid." The female officer shook her head as my escorts left. Maybe she heard my mother crying. I watched their backs and only knew they were leaving the drabness of the county jail, walking outside, not even twenty feet, to where the freedom I couldn't touch shone bright under the sun. I was falling deeper and deeper into a hole I'd dug myself into but couldn't dig myself out of. If I'd seen that hole three months before, I would have run away from the man sleeping in his car. As I looked around the jail, I realized that my days as a juvenile were done. And they were. Once you were in the system there wasn't anything saying you came in as a kid. You were just in, shut out with the light of day. All I had behind me were the snatches of small talk exchanged with guards before court dates, where they heard twelve million black voices crying out to a juvenile court judge for mercy. They were tired of the parade.

2

Things I Know and Don't Know
About My Father

My father is a convicted felon. He is a smart man and went to college, Old Dominion University. Because he lived in D.C. and no one has ever told me I come from rich people, he must have gotten a scholarship. He could swim for days, and for years taught people to swim with the public parks and recreation folks. He never taught me to swim, to throw a left hand—or to value the way something you say can make people pay attention. I couldn't tell you the name of my father's father. I am told that my grandfather was the son of a Cherokee woman, but I couldn't prove it. My grandfather could bump into me on an empty street in any city in America and I wouldn't recognize him. And even though I've met my mother's father, the only things I know about the man is that I've never seen him in a room with my grandmother and he loves James Brown. The men in my family had disappeared before I was old enough to know they were missing, and if the wrong person speaks he will cite that as the reason why I went to prison. Something in my blood that turns foolishness into felonies. That's what I thought about when I walked into the jail. If I wanted to talk I talked to myself. I couldn't tell you the name of anyone in my family older than fifty-five the morning I was arrested. But I never told a judge, a lawyer or a cop anything about myself. The only thing that was important to them was the gun I pulled on the man sleeping in his car, and I understood that. The circumstance of the crime, the color of the jacket I wore and even the caliber pistol I held were only important in the way they contributed to me walking into Fairfax County Jail with cuffs on.

One day the juvenile court judge asked, "Are you aware your charges carry a life sentence in adult court?" The only person in the crowd I knew was my mother. She'd taken off work, and every time the lawyer or the judge spoke to me, they were speaking to her. And every time the judge mentioned my crime, my mom's face said I was crushing her. The crowd got quiet when the judge asked his question. I wanted to ask him what he thought I could do with a life sentence. A life sentence puts age into perspective. It meant that I wouldn't shovel snow from the sidewalk before my mother's house again, that I wouldn't dribble my basketball down Silver Hill Road on the way to the library. It meant the sisters I'd met just before getting locked up, the ones who stood bright-eyed and anxious as I talked to my father for the first time in twelve years, wouldn't know my favorite ice cream was butter pecan, and my mother would spend more time than she had wondering where she went wrong. I have no idea where my father was when the judge spoke to me.

I ignored everyone who tried to warn me away from the streets. I thought there was an imaginary line that would keep me safe. If I stood on corners but didn't sell crack I'd be okay. If I smoked weed but did well in school I'd be okay. I couldn't wrap my mind around a life sentence, but I'd walked into a world where I was either a good kid or a super predator that the world had to fear. I'd walked into a world where people looked at me the way they looked at my father. Maybe. It's hard to construct a life off scraps, off loose pieces of information. I heard my father jumped out of a third-floor window and walked away. That he once pulled a machete on a man in anger. I heard these stories after I was locked up. Before prison, my father got judged by his absence. It was almost the way the judge judged me, except the judge was concerned with my presence. All he needed to know was that there was a witness who said I'd pulled a gun on him and a police detective who agreed. Those were the facts that said life sentence.

That's not this story though; it's not about my father being absent or the stories about the men in my family I don't know. That story is an old story. I saw it played out in the streets when the streetlights still signaled that I needed to go inside. It's on the news, in books. Close your eyes and hear sirens wail as cops draw guns and somebody's brother, son, husband is going away in cuffs. *To cuff* is to smack someone upside the head or slam steel bracelets over their wrists. Anyone who doesn't know the story of cuffs and black men can walk into any juvenile detention center in America, any jail or any prison and see the same thing: a rack of black bodies. Men walking around those small confined spaces like they own them, because in a way they do. The time behind bars connected me to the lives of black men, to their stories and their silences. I found my father's life somewhere behind bars.

My father and I share a history of not knowing. And this history is more important, in a way, than the one I have with the family I know—because the only one who knows what the inside of a jail cell smells like is him. My father knows that there was a man I'd made a victim. What I've never told him is this: there was a victim and there was that night his eyes opened wider than silver dollars. I had a pistol in my palm for the first time. And I knew that meant nothing. I knew that if he ever spoke, he would tell the judge how I looked like the man who had pointed a pistol toward his forehead. He would say he thought about his mother as he got out of the car, and that he thought about his girlfriend. He would tell the judge he thought about his daughter, if he had one. If he spoke, he would have talked about imagining his life ending as a bullet smashed through his skull, and he would say that as he stepped out of the car he thought it was a joke. If he talked, I would have listened, and maybe even known that there was nothing I could say that would make sense to my mother after he spoke.

I was in the jail because I'd been certified as an adult. I doubt my father knew what that meant in 1996. My mother didn't know. My grandmother didn't know, and none of my aunts knew. It was more new vocabulary. Ask someone how many juveniles are in prisons or jails doing time with adults. Most people will look at you like you've said something crazy. They don't know that there were at least a dozen juveniles at Fairfax County Jail the morning I arrived. *Certified.* It's a legal hocus-pocus where the prosecuting attorney made my sixteen-year-old body an adult by the signing of a paper. Truth is, I confessed before the police talked to me for ten minutes. I tried to lie, to talk my way out of it. But, in the end, all I did was confess.

3

Fairfax County Jail: R Cells

n the jail a woman passed by me with fake eyelashes and the brown uniform of a deputy tight as skin on her body. From where they left me, I saw a group of men gathered around waiting to get mug shots. The mug shot declared that I was property of the state. The stamp. Without it, I had a sinner's chance of leaving the jail without the burden of cuffs. The mug shot made the reality of my one day going to prison real. Up until then the shuttling back and forth into courtrooms seemed a formality to my release. Believing that I would go home is an insanity that I recognize now. But then I thought it was possible to confess to carjacking and have a court let you walk away with a *my bad*. A do-over. It doesn't so much matter now. I was even cuffed while they snapped the picture of me, caught up trying to test just how far into the streets I could step without becoming their victim.

The handcuffs on my wrists reminded me of freedom, and the jail meant having on handcuffs even when I didn't have on handcuffs. It meant always waiting to be moved from cell to cell but never from cell to home. The deputy taking my mug shot didn't need much time to tell me to get back on the bench, but it took at least two more hours before someone called out, "Betts, you're moving into an R cell." R cells: a few walkways of one-man cells in the basement of the Fairfax County Jail. There men shouted for everything and nothing. On the doors screaming at one another about what they lost and what they had left. I walked alone even though a deputy led me to the jail cell that was empty of everything but the grit and grime of all the men who had laid their bones on the concrete that served as a bed. Alone . . . and all I could do was close my eyes and imagine how much time the judge would give me. The sound of the cell door closing was another closed fist upside my head, and it was only after that that the guard reached into the tray slot of the cell and uncuffed my hands.

The jail cell was the barest room I'd ever seen, the walls not white but a mix of brown, yellow and the peeling of age. It reeked. The deputy walked away from me without speaking. All he left me with was a blanket that would cover half my five-foot-six-inch frame if I stretched it. He had to come back and give me a blanket is what I thought. That's why I didn't yell out to him, didn't remind him that I didn't have sheet or mattress or real blanket. I expected to get a mattress, to be treated as if I deserved not to sleep in a cold cell on a cold slab of concrete in the dead of winter. Although it was cold I peeled my sweater off. When I threw the colorful mess onto the slab of concrete that was my bed, it landed on dried spit.

Days passed and I still had no mattress. It was February and cold, and I hadn't changed my clothes since walking into the jail.

"Deputy! Deputy! Ay, look man, look in this cell. I need a mattress, a pillow. All y'all left me with is this small-ass blanket."

The deputy didn't stop walking, but he looked in my direction.

"How long you been in there?"

He moved along as he asked his question, then stopped and walked back toward me. I thought, if he looks in here he'll be able to see that I smell like I've been living in a puddle of piss and sleeping on cold concrete. "I've been here about three, four days. Deputy, I haven't had a shower, no phone call. This ain't right. You gotta do something for me." I was begging and learning Prison 101. You could beg, but that just made you feel like the time was doing you, like you weren't in control of yourself. Worse than that, you could beg and still not get anything. I didn't get a mattress that day, and after asking for a day or so longer gave up on it. I learned to ignore the night air as it cut into my skin, ignore the indents and ridges of the concrete scraping my face; I learned a little bit about how to say fuck everything and still look forward to a tomorrow.

Just about every deputy I saw in those first few days at the jail was white. Every judge was white, and even if it made no sense I was seeing the world along color lines. The thing was, part of me wouldn't let me reduce my being locked up to something about race. I had no problem reducing moments to race when cuffs were tightened a little too tough, or those nights in the R cell without a mattress. There were times when I knew that if I was a young white boy I wouldn't even have been in the jail. But part of me knew that it was the gun in my hand and that man sleeping in his car that made my mother sad. The night at the Springfield mall landed me in the cell, and in a way it didn't matter that I didn't have a mattress. I knew that if I hadn't robbed that man I wouldn't have been in the R cell and wouldn't have been wearing the same underwear for all the days that I was checking off with scratch marks in the wall. The funk from my clothes taught me that in prison you aren't shit. And the population scared me, so while the lack of a mattress frustrated me, fear always trumped frustration. I'd learned to deal with the cold, the cutting concrete. I didn't know then how I'd deal with the men in population.

One day I heard a thumping on my cell wall. The cell was bare save for the concrete slab that served as a bed and the tin toilet and sink combination that leaned against the wall. There weren't any bars, but a sort of iron mesh that reminded me of what people put over the first-floor apartment windows where I'd lived as a young kid. "A Yo, Yo." The voice called out my cell number. "Cell Nine!" I didn't know him, but needed another voice. Talking to myself was getting old fast.

"What's up?"

"Nothing, man. I heard you over there yelling about a mattress. You don't have a mattress?"

To talk we had to scream through the small crack in the cell's door. "Nah. No pillow either. And I been in here for a minute. The deputies saying fuck me, so I'm sleeping on the concrete."

"Shit. They call me Chi. I been down here for a couple of weeks, and it's been rough, but at least I got a mattress."

Chi told me his story. Spilled his guts, you could say, to a person he'd never seen. And I wasn't but half interested. Chi told me about gangs—his gang in particular—and how a fight at his high school turned into an attempted murder charge. While he talked I slipped my fingers through the grill that covers the cell door. Chi was younger than me. Just fifteen. He thought he was going home, too. Told me he wasn't guilty, but I knew that if I couldn't understand his story of being in a gang but not being in a gang, and almost being in the fight but not having the knife, the judge wouldn't understand it. Judges learned to read our complexions, crimes and communities as reasons why we needed the bars of a jail. And anyone telling me that isn't true should take a look at the shades of brown I watched walk in and out of the system. Couldn't tell me then this wasn't true, when I'd seen one white child locked up in three months. Chi told me he wasn't guilty, and I told him it probably didn't matter. That was the first time I'd spent more than a moment at the door.

Across from my cell was the section of padded cells. Chi had become my source of information on the jail. He told me the officers at Fairfax were known for beating *locos* down. His English was spattered with Spanish words I mostly didn't know, but I got that one and wondered if the pun was intended. *Locos:* slang for homie, brother, friend in Spanish, but literally meaning crazy. The padded cells were designated for the people who were a danger to themselves or someone else. Chi said, "You either crazy when they put you in there or crazy when they bring you out." I wanted to know how he knew, but before I asked he told me that he watched them strip somebody and throw him in there. Neither one of us had been locked up long, but we both knew it didn't matter what the naked man did. It only mattered that he was a little too loud on the wrong day and that a deputy willing to do the paperwork got him tossed into one of the padded cells on GP. General principle. Just because the badge said he could.

It was February then, with the cold beating back against the day and me shivering in the cell for hours at a time. I talked for hours to someone I'd never seen before because we were both starving for a human voice. People screamed day and night just to be heard, thinking that the hearing made them human. I built two days around Chi's voice. Waiting to hear him thump on the wall beside me to start a conversation. It kept me from thinking about how I would scream in a room with a straitjacket on. It kept me from thinking about what a person did to himself to make the deputies stop trusting him with silverware and toilet paper. The padded cell scared me, made me not want to ask for a mattress, to push too hard, because I'd built a scenario in my head where I was tossed into a padded cell for demanding a mattress. That's what prison did to my young mind. It made me rationalize cruelty; it made me think that everything mocked me, even the dim light that never went out.

DAYDREAMING

This is what I told myself most days: I'm five feet six inches or so and can pace the entire cell lengthwise in three short steps, one long. When I jump the ceiling still hangs just outside my reach. I jump to test my boundaries, reach up and see how much the cell contains me. It contains me fully. But I keep jumping, I'm a trapped animal measuring my confinement as if effort will bring down these walls, as if I'll jump, and for one second become Magic Johnson after he found out he had HIV. So I fantasize like a kid. It's the last second of the NBA all-star game and I have the rock. I pump fake, jab step and then take two dribbles to the right. The crowd erupts when I jump. The ball is released; it's headed in. It swishes. When I land on my feet I'm still in the cell. The crowd is a bunch of men hollering for food and telephones and attention. Ain't shit changed, this cell more like a cage than anything else, or a fist closing around my sanity. And I'm dreaming on my feet, playacting like I'm still a kid. Lost in it, too, just like you get lost in a dream, with everything bleeding into itself until what's real and fake isn't important, so much as what you see, and all I see is the ceiling just outside my reach.

4

Will You Accept This Call?

When I had the phone, I called everyone. Whoever's number I remembered picked up the phone to a voice saying, "You have a collect call from the Fairfax County Jail, if you'd like to accept this call please dial one." One night my aunt Samantha told me the story of Terrence Johnson. How he'd gotten locked up when he was fifteen. Sent to prison. She didn't tell me what he was locked up for, that he'd rocked the Prince George's County community the night he shot and killed two police officers. He and his brother had been picked up for suspicion of breaking into a Laundromat coin box. His brother Daryl was seventeen. It was 1978 and the PG police were rumored to beat people down and ask questions later. Terrence insisted that the police beat him down, and that he reached for an officer's gun in desperation. Before the night ended two officers were dead and the gun was still smoking in Terrence's hand. That night my aunt Samantha was feeding me the facts that made me think I could make it, because Terrence got a degree in prison and was at home attending the University of the District of Columbia's law school. I stowed that little bit of information in my head. It didn't make the R cells any easier, didn't make the slab any less rough. It just meant that things could get better.

My aunt didn't know that Terrence Johnson fired a bullet into his own head. The news reports say that the pressure got to him. His brother says he was waiting on a book contract, that he had run up bills and needed money to pay them and support his wife and child. He'd lost his scholarship. None of the reports I read said that he couldn't deal with freedom after spending his childhood staring out of jail cells, but that's what I thought had happened. That no matter what, he couldn't run from nights alone with his crime. I learned his story and told myself I wasn't going out like that.

"Get dressed, you're going to see the nurse," a deputy called into the cell. Seeing the nurse meant I'd be going to population soon. You couldn't go to the jail population without seeing the nurse. This was around my eighth day in the R cell. I hadn't had a shower in over a week and smelled like it. When I walked into the nurse's office, the staff stepped back. I'd gotten bored in the cell and had been masturbating every day for a good week. Twice a day, maybe three or four times. I was testing out the theory that excessive masturbation would drive you mad. What was I supposed to do? Locked up in a cell alone for the first time with no windows, no mattress, no sheets. My mind was banging against the walls. No other truth but that, my mind banging up against the four walls of a jail cell and fifteen seconds of pleasure all I could look forward to. A cell will make you crazier than masturbation any day, and I wasn't going to explain how funky I was to the two white women that stood before me. A jail cell will take away a man's shame, make him wear *fuck the world* on his forehead and in the makeshift scowl he learns to carry on his face.

"Ms. I been in that cell for eight days. No shower, no change of clothes, no mattress. I'm saying—"

Two nurses in the room. I don't know if they were sympathetic or not, but they didn't let me finish talking. They wouldn't talk to me until I took a shower, my smell more offensive to them than anything I had to say. Afterward they listened to the story and demanded I get a mattress. Someone reading this might think of the women as my heroes; they weren't. They taught me that you only had power in jail if someone moved after you spoke, that having a voice was never enough, and I resented that bit of truth. It was as if I would have rather continued to suffer, even though I know that's not the truth. It reminded me of what I thought a gun in my hand said about power. How something that weighed next to nothing in my palm added a ton to the tenor of my voice, made every word I said matter. Every day taught me how not to let what I didn't have break me. I talked to my folks and acted like all was normal, or I talked to them and didn't tell them that I hadn't changed my clothes in a week, that I hadn't seen a bar of soap in a week. I never told them about what it means to have cold bury itself in your bones.

The nurses looked shocked to learn I was sixteen. I'd only been locked up for a few months, but all the shock had left me. I thought shit just happened.

When the guard came to take me back to the cell I was different. Fresh from a twenty-minute shower and in a uniform that would remind me and everyone else that I was incarcerated. A pair of green pants and a shirt. What surprised me was that my bag of property and a slip to order commissary came with my mattress. The ten dollars and change I had in my pocket when I got locked up had been placed on my account. It was money I'd taken from the man I'd robbed. Ten dollars had me in a jail cell facing a life sentence. That's irony for you, sacrificed my life for less money than I could have bummed on a corner. I spent the money on junk food. Brownies, Skittles, Snickers, Moon Pies. Nothing but junk food.

They'd given me the only paperback book that was in my property. *Going to Meet the Man* by James Baldwin. I started reading Baldwin because I saw his books on my friend Tameka's mother's bookshelf. I called my mother and she cried on the phone. She didn't tell me I'd hurt her, she just cried and asked if I was okay. The title story of Baldwin's book was about a cop who couldn't get over a lynching he'd seen. Baldwin writes that they burned the body and there were women and children watching. That people got souvenirs. Fingers, pieces of bone. The cop was a boy when the lynching happened and he was on his father's shoulders. The book didn't make me angry. It made me think I knew something about the way the world worked and what was behind the way the deputies looked into my eyes. I learned about the world by reading the authors on Tameka's mother's shelf. J. California Cooper, Baldwin, Chinua Achebe. And I rarely told anyone what I read. I lived with a secret world going on inside my head and suddenly I was locked up in a place where the secret world was becoming the only reality that made sense. At the detention center my mother brought me an armful of books each week. Walter Mosley, Sherlock Holmes and any other mystery she could find. My grandmother brought me Kahlil Gibran.

Two hours before the Baldwin book added weight to my empty palms, I was a sixteen-year-old black boy smelling like a week's worth of piss, used to sleeping on a concrete slab with spit and who knows what else dried up on it. The book didn't make me anything more than that, but it let me curl up inside my own mind and be free.

The print on the pages gave me a world far from mine that still had the feel of my world. Reading was what I needed to beat back all that noise and silence, those horrible silences. Once I had the book, I held my complaints close to my chest. I didn't know what was waiting for me in population.

5

Halfway to Hell

arly one morning a man shouted for the phone for an hour, then he shouted for Jesus. I felt bad for him. A few hours later a deputy told me, "You're going to B-five, the third cell from the front door."

Leaving the cell made me think about my first cell. Being in jail, in prison, is nothing but a series of cells. White. Hospital white. Or mental institution white. It felt clean, but that didn't matter. The first cellmate I ever had was Peanut. He told me he'd spent the past five or six Christmases in a cell. Not that he'd been locked up for five years, just that the holiday season seemed to always find him in a cage. Nothing but a kid like me, but spending just as much time in a cell as at home. For fighting, for not going to school. Little stuff that you'd think someone would have helped him deal with all the time he spent locked up. They didn't help him deal with anything though, just helped him learn a new way to measure freedom and time.

"You're lucky you're going to the second floor. All the kids go there. It's calmer than the third floor, and you're not ready for the fourth floor," the deputy told me as we waited for the elevator to open again. He was black with a crooked mustache. The right half dipped as if it wanted to be a goatee, while the rest was army-thin. It didn't take me but a week to see a difference in the deputies. The white ones only spoke to order me around. They weren't mean, or rude, just silent. Most times, though, the black deputies would speak. When we made it to our stop, I was thankful to be getting out of the elevator with him. I eased my bag from over my right shoulder.

"This is it here, just go in and pick a cell. You can pick which cell you want. It's only you and one other boy in here." I thought to myself: what I look like picking my own cell. I told him, "Whichever." From a panel at the front he controlled the cell doors. I noticed, but it wasn't important, it wasn't like he was going to let me borrow the key one day. A letter marked each cell. Five cells, five letters. A-B-C-D-E. He put me in cell D. I fingered the white band they'd tied around my arm, a hospital band, with my last name and a number on it, 90673. That number was more important than my name. I gave it to my moms so she could put it on the letters she wrote to me. If a letter came in the mail for Dwayne Betts, it didn't mean a thing. In jail, in prison, names are meaningless. It's always the number that marks you. The number that you can't run from.

"There's one other person in the block with you. Each morning, at eight a.m., you have to come out of your cell and stay in the block until five in the afternoon. You can watch whatever you want on TV." He talked, and then left. If I had a question it wasn't important. There were two showers with ragged green curtains near the front door of the cellblock and two toilets separated by a brick wall between them with nothing covering them from the front. The wall rose to just above my waist.

When I walked out of my cell in the morning I wanted to cry, or fight. I hadn't cried since my second day locked up. The morning after we were arrested deputies came to take us to court. It was a

juvenile court and in the holding cell with us were four young brothers. My co-defendant's name was Brandon and if I said anything to
him as we prepared to go into court it's lost in my head. *Co-defendant*
wasn't an SAT word. It wasn't a word that I'd ever used in my life but
suddenly, Brandon, my friend, was my co-defendant. The holding
cell had rusted bars that I gripped while I waited to be called. What I
remember is someone told us that everyone goes home on their par-
ents' recognizance for their first charge. *Recognizance*, another one
of those words I learned from trouble. It meant that my moms would
agree to bring me before court on the scheduled date. That's what
someone said; they said it was a *lock*. A *lock* as in a guarantee. I'd be
going home for Christmas, and then take care of this little business
after the holidays is what they had me thinking. How was I to know
that everyone locked up wants to be an expert about something? I
needed the young boys with cornrows and knotty heads like mine
to try to calm me down with the magic of the word *recognizance*.

I knew the judge wasn't aware of their pep talk when he told the
courtroom, "The defendant will be held in the custody of the state
until his next court date." He might as well have hit me with the gavel
and split my head open to the white meat. I thought he was kidding,
especially when he set the next court date for after the New Year.
When I found out he told Brandon the same thing moments after
that, I knew it was true. We were in that holding cell again, waiting
to be taken back to Landmark, when I started crying. Sixteen and
I hadn't missed a Christmas in my life. This was the first time that
going to jail meant more than push-ups and spades games; the first
time that it meant missing something. It crushed me. Tears covered
my face. It was so bad the person locked in the cell with us wanted
to offer advice. He'd been through the system before, I guess. All I
remember about him are the cornrows in his hair, in a fancy design
that I don't think you can get in a jail.

"Let me give y'all the game" is what he said with the authority of someone who'd been there. "When you go back to court, tell them that you were high. Tell them that you bought some boat from Mookie from Arlington. You know it's ten niggas named Mookie from Arlington. You'll get a drug program. It's both of your first charges, right?" We nodded, in tears. But you know, none of that stuff was true. I'd already told them I was guilty, I wasn't going to be high, too. I wasn't ready to tell a judge that I was off the boat, to tell my mother that I was running wild in the streets with PCP hijacking my common sense.

There were scratches on the wall near my cell that I stared at after lockdown. I spent three days in the juvenile block watching television and sitting across from a kid my age who wouldn't say more than three words in any one day. I worked out. Fifty push-ups in sets of ten. I called myself getting strong, thought if I was going to be anything it would be heavier than one hundred twenty-six pounds when I found out what would happen to me.

Each morning the deputies locked us out of our cells. The only school they had in the jail was GED offered to all inmates, and since at that time we couldn't be around adults, we couldn't go to school. We had Jerry Springer, Ricki Lake and all the other morning talk shows to educate us. We had soap operas and afternoon cartoons. The only time the boy locked up with me broke his silence was to tell me he set fires. He didn't tell me what he set on fire, just said, "They caught me setting fires," as if that explained it all.

I had two visits while in the juvenile block. When my mother came to Fairfax County Jail, a guard opened the front door of the cellblock and yelled, "Betts, you have a visitor." The first time it happened I couldn't run out of the block fast enough. A deputy stopped me as I approached the visiting area and asked for my pass, the small white piece of paper given to me as I left. A pass. A note that said it was okay for me to walk the halls. I showed him. "Wait here," he told me and walked through a door. When he came back, he led me into a room that was more a single hallway with a bunch of stalls than a room. "Sit at number eight." Each stall had a stool bolted to the ground, a piece of Plexiglas separating the jail side from the free and a phone dangling from its cord. That's when I learned the term *noncontact visit*.

I talked about food with my moms. About my cousins, about the weather. We didn't talk about the crime, about the courts. I'd told her I was guilty and now guilt wasn't as important as my safety. I'd been locked up long enough for the people who had been asking her about me to stop, and so the small talk was a way for me to get included in the lives that I was missing. The birthdays, the arguments. In the end, my moms always wanted to know how I was. Even though I told her how I hated the block and that the boy in there with me had something wrong with him. She wanted to know how I was and I told her bored. But I was away from everyone else, and that's what made her feel a bit of peace. Given the kid sharing the block with me, I may as well have been by myself. Even when I told her that I wondered how long it would last. No one at the jail had spoken to me.

6

A Need for Space

One morning a deputy came to the block and told us we were moving. Behind the move was a need for space. "Get your stuff together," the deputy told us. My trash bag was again filled with my property. I carried everything I owned around like a homeless man. This time the deputy didn't lead us anywhere. He gave us the number of a block and expected us to walk there, straight there. And I did. I had nowhere else to go and there wasn't anywhere to hide. The hallways, empty for a minute as I walked, were the only place in the jail that the sun touched. I might have been leaving the relative safety of a juvenile block, but I knew I'd have gone crazy in there. They didn't let us go to the library, there was no school and there were only the two of us in the cellblock. I was scared, with tight knots forming in my stomach, but glad to be getting away from the solitude of the R cells and the two-man juvenile block.

There was a deputy station before each cellblock. The female deputy was the first I'd noticed as more than a brown suit. "How you doing?" I asked her. She made me notice that the hair on my face had grown thicker, not thick enough to see, but thick enough to make my mustache visible without straining your eyes. I thought she was too fine to be working in a jail.

"What's your name?" When she asked me I thought she was flirting. Hers was the closest thing to a kind face that I'd seen. The uniform she wore was the same brown as everyone else's. It was the military, except the war they fought was to keep us locked up. And as fine as she was that was her job, to make sure I was where I should be, in cuffs or in a cellblock. I stared at her until she said again, "Your name?"

"I'm sorry. Dwayne." She told me there was no Dwayne on the list. No Dwayne Betts either when I added my last name. That's when I realized that she was looking for Reginald. Reginald is my daddy's name, and neither then nor now do I give it as mine. "Reginald." Reginald I told her. Reginald Betts. She shook her head, opened the cellblock door and told me that I was in cell C. It was the morning, so she only let me into the cell to sit my stuff down. You got locked out of your cell in the adult blocks, too. I thought the deputies were running game on the juveniles by locking us out of the cell during the daytime. That morning I realized the game was on everyone with a number attached to their name. They told grown men when and for how long they could stay in their cell. It was spitting in our faces. We'd forfeited our freedom through crime or we were fighting to prove we were innocent of crimes, and still we were treated like dogs you put out in the morning to piss and shit on the lawn.

I walked into the block and people didn't stop what they were doing. Someone laughed. "Slim, they put someone in the cell with you." I threw my stuff on the bed lying on the floor in the cell that split the small block in half. The cell was like an R cell, except with a mattress on the floor it seemed smaller. One man slept on a mattress on a concrete slab, the other slept on the floor. There was a small light above a little table at the back of the cell that always stayed on. The room was so tiny that both of us couldn't rightly stand at the same time. No wonder they kept us out of the cell during the day. For a minute I just stood there looking around. Every day was a reminder of how my situation grew from bad to worse.

"Betts, get out of the cell," the female deputy yelled at me. I'd been in there for two seconds and already she was screaming on me. Power worked that way in the jail. The brown suits ready to tell you when you were wrong without a second thought, and what could we say back? Talk a little trash like the drunks in the basement or the late-night hollerers? No one heard them. I didn't say a thing. Threw on my mad face and eased out of the cell to look around the narrow block. Nine men around me. The natty-headed one with the ragged facial hair was doing push-ups. In front of him was a dude with his sleeves rolled up to show how big his arms were.

Four brothers were at the picnic table watching the soaps. I'd learn that you didn't touch the TV from twelve to four p.m. That was soap opera time. Before that was talk show time, and after that was cartoon time. Nights were up for grabs unless basketball or football was on. Sports trumped everything. When I walked in no one looked up from what they were doing. There were three Latinos there. The block wasn't big enough for all of us. People didn't move around too much to keep from standing on top of each other.

"What's up, youngin?" I turned around, back toward the door that was closing. The natty-headed dude said, "My name Dred, man." He wiped his hand off on his torn sweatpants and offered it. A handshake, not dap like we gave on the street, and for a moment the two of us weren't in a cellblock but somewhere else. Outside of a church, or a school, a place where black men shake each other's hands when they meet. And then, before I could say my name, we were back in prison, a place where black men go to meet each other's pain.

"Dwayne. Dwayne." I told him my name twice, as if I wasn't sure it was me there, in the pod at that moment. If I tell you I was shaking I'd be lying. I'm sure no one knew I was scared, nervous or nothing like that. But the first few moments in a new place, whether it was a detention center, a jail cell, a block—the first few moments threatened to explode with whatever would happen after that. I always felt like I was waiting for the explosion. Dred asked, "You want to get in on this?"

I told him I was cool. Appreciated the offer, but said no because I didn't know him. I didn't know it then but push-ups would become my main source of recreation, and I'd learn more ways to do push-ups than most black folks know how to cook chicken. Just to know, I called out, "How many are you doing, anyway?"

Dred told me that he was doing two hundred and Damien, the youngin who pulled the sleeves of his short-sleeve shirt up between each set to show people he had muscles, was doing four hundred. Four hundred of the ugliest push-ups I'd ever seen, but four hundred. His body wasn't straight like my uncle Sam made us do. And I wasn't anywhere near the afternoons when I struggled through ten push-ups because my uncle thought they'd make a man of me, or because it was the only punishment he'd gotten from his Marine Corps years that were suited for a teenager. Damien's back curved toward the ground like he was doing the snake as just his arms maintained a normal movement. I heard him telling Dred that push-ups like that focus the work on the arms. I didn't believe him, and even though I wanted to get a couple of sets in, I walked toward the picnic table and sat in a chair, half listening to the soaps.

One morning before breakfast, Dred pushed his door open ten minutes after I'd opened mine. I sat near him and asked him where he was from.

"Where I'm from? What the fuck you mean where I'm from? What the bumba clot kind of question is that? I'm from the city." I should have expected him to say that—there was a fascination in the jail with being from D.C. People claimed "the city" as if it was one place, all they needed was an aunt, brother, sister or cousin that once upon a time lived there and they walked around as if they had some mythical reputation from the streets. In jails and prisons you can be from anywhere you want, and you can be anyone you want, as long as your fists can back it up.

It started as a joke. Damien, Dred, Richard and Chris would be playing cards. Playing spades. A spades game is theater in jail. This is what the couple people I knew at home talked about when they came back from prison. Talked about spades and push-ups as if that was all being locked up was about, and they had good reason. Give four men that can't breathe free air fifty-two cards and a table and you'll see high drama enacted. It might have started with Chris at the table yelling, "Young blood, tell this nigga that bitch ain't no good at this table," as he slammed a low spade on Dred's queen of hearts, or it might have started with Richard throwing a spade face-down on the first club play, waiting for someone to turn it over as if it was dynamite. Whatever the case it always started, someone in the game drawing someone outside of the game into it. I spent months in the same block. Learned about the game of spades there and how it could turn the years I might have to do into a series of moments where I prayed I ended up with the last trump. Most days, the same people played spades and talked the same shit. When Chris called me young blood, it started this freestyle about my age. As Damien shuffled the cards he told the table that I was so young he could still smell Similac on my breath and that I couldn't know what grown folks were doing with the fifty-two that he held in his hand. "This muthafucka a kid, man. That's why he ain't playing with us now, he's trying to learn. Matter fact, get next D."

That's just how it went at the card table. By the time I started playing, we'd realized that Damien had been beating us in the head the whole time. He was cheating, stashing all the high spades on the bottom of the deck and then dealing them to himself. First time I actually saw someone deal from the bottom of the deck. His hands moved so fast you only saw it if you knew what you were looking for. The okeydoke. His cheating was changing the rules of the game but no one knew but him. The judges did the same thing to most of the brothers going to court. Before they went in, everyone to a man guessed their sentence wrong. They didn't understand the logic of presentencing reports and witnesses crying, it was just like the system was dealing from the bottom of the deck, and you only peeped it if you knew what to look for in advance. That's what I thought then, watching Damien deal from the bottom even though we knew his trick. At the card table he could be the system for a minute, rigging the game even if the people playing knew it.

The first Latino I talked to in the jail wore Chuck Taylors. Droopy got his Chucks the same morning I got the white Converse basketball shoes. Droopy could draw. He made the corner of an envelope look like a rose you could touch. He sold the envelopes after sketching flowers on them in pen ink. I bought a couple for Mom and her sisters. Droopy showed me how to draw them, how to brush the tip of the pen against the envelope's corner, shading the flower. Sometimes mine came out good, but mostly they didn't. Mostly it was just another way to watch a day go by. Half the names in the block drifted out of my mind as people shuffled in and out. Even the names of my cell partners faded. Sometimes a new person came into the cell every week. And I forgot them because they didn't have any time, weren't facing any time or just didn't have interesting things to say. However, I did find myself talking to people I would never have spoken to under other circumstances.

But there was still the chaos of trash talking and time. One night the whole block could hear Dred yelling. "This nigga pussy for real," he said, pointing at the new dude, Joe. He'd been in the block for a week and lied almost every time he opened his mouth. Once, at the card table, crimes had come up. I didn't talk about my crime often; it carried a life sentence and I didn't want to be the center of the "how much time you think he going to get" questions. That day, though, when someone asked I said carjacking. Joe said, "Shit, I remember the first time I carjacked somebody. We was looking for a van to do this hit with and shit, so we was out cruising the city. I saw this old man pulling up at a light . . . when I walked up on him, he tried to yell. I laid his ass down 'cause I didn't want to leave any witnesses. Youngin, you shouldn't have left no witnesses."

People call jails college campuses for criminals. The idea being that people come to jail and leave better able to jimmy a lock, pick a pocket or stand on a corner selling dime bags all day. I thought about that as I listened to Joe's lies multiply into crimes for which any judge with open eyes would hand out a dozen life sentences. Before a few days had passed he'd bragged about catching bodies, carjackings, armed robberies, assaults, kidnappings and just about every other crime a judge could name. He was the purest of liars, Michael Jordan dumping in free throws with his eyes closed for hundred-dollar bills. How was that teaching me to become a better criminal? Joe told me he didn't believe in leaving witnesses behind. His words were dangerous that way. They wouldn't have made me a better criminal if I believed him and his laundry list of felonies; they would have made me a depraved one who didn't give a fuck about anything. That was the real problem with jails and with the impressionable folks in them. They soaked up Joe's lies like he was Jesse James and they might have tried to live them out. Who knows, maybe I was living out someone's lie, gun in hand, the night I carjacked the sleeping man.

Dred called Joe pussy because one day he was tired of hearing his lies. He said, "All I know is the muthafucka say he from D.C., but ain't no niggas like that from D.C." Dred believed there was a D.C. type, a mythical half-man/half-gangster who hailed from the potholes in the streets. The irony was, if there was a D.C. type, Joe probably fit it. He talked like he was from the city, he knew the street names, the go-go bands and he could play ball. Dred was just talking, because whatever Joe was, he knew twice as much about D.C. as Dred. And when Joe called Dred out, nothing happened. It was just a shouting match teaching me how talking tough didn't mean anything. All the *bitch niggas* and stories about what they would do to each other simply gave the rest of us in the block comedy, more drama for the people in the block, beaten back by the thought of time, to live off of until the next moment.

Some entire days went by without the tension that sat like a cloud above the block threatening a storm, but some days the signs of an approaching storm were all anyone could see. I could see it in Droopy's blank face as he sat on the brick by the telephone. I could see it in the way Richard and Chris banged bones on the table as they each took turns calling out domino. It rang out in arguments over the TV and the phone. I should have been able to predict how the rest of the day would go.

Damien walked over to me and I knew he was ready to start playing too much. Some people, in an effort to beat back the boredom, would try to make somebody their personal amusement. It would be subtle, the smallest people in the block were most susceptible. Never all the way malicious, it would begin with slap boxing or wrestling or shooting the dozens back and forth. Most times it even stayed there, but depending on what kind of game was being run, and how far the person running game thought he could stretch it, the slap boxing could become beating somebody into a corner, taking their food or worse. I wasn't worried about Damien, but I watched where he took it and had been feeling like he was pushing me too far. I felt like if I was his brother, none of the stuff happening would be a big deal; but I wasn't his brother.

"What you know about D.C., young blood? You calling Joe a liar." Damien wasn't looking at me. He was looking at Joe and at Dred. He started talking to both of them, taking the focus from their argument and putting it on me. He wanted someone to tell him what I learned about the streets from reading books. He called me choirboy. I didn't respond, but when someone is talking to you in jail, silence isn't worth a copper nickel. He took my silence as the cue to keep going. I stared out the one window onto the street. I had to strain my eyes to see a person from that height. Without my glasses I could hardly make out the faces before me. I'd learned to recognize people from the way they talked and their mannerisms. If they had hair on their face or if they always brought a hand to their face before talking. But even with twenty-twenty vision you had to touch the bars with your nose to see the streets below us. I saw more bars and sky than people, freedom and jail before my eyes, as behind me Damien thought that there was an invisible string on my back that he pulled for his amusement. When I got off the ledge that let me look out the window, Damien threw his hands up and tossed a lightweight jab into the air.

I told him, "Go ahead, young. I ain't playing around." Damien had been pulling me into his play fights for a while, sometimes at night, after they opened up the cells and it got more boring than usual. It would be Dred, Damien, me, Droopy and Richard in the block. For a while Dred and Damien would slap box and then I'd get pulled into it. I probably let myself get pulled in; the play was a way for me to practice for when I had to throw a punch meant to hit someone.

"Throw your hands up, nigga!" he called out that day, pushing me too far. I caught his left with my right forearm. He wasn't trying to hit me anyway, his fist still half open. I backed up even though I blocked the punch. Backed up until I was almost at the phone in the corner by the concrete slab Droopy sat on.

"Why you keep fucking with him," Droopy said. When I turned, Droopy held his ink pen like a knife, plucking bits of dirt and lint from under his nails.

"Who the fuck you talking to?" Damien's face turned red. He didn't see that the little Puerto Rican had gotten up from his seat across the block by the television. Droopy wasn't saying anything. He looked up, his pen in his hand. "I'm talking to you," and he jumped off the wall.

In a minute it was over. No one argued and the Puerto Rican had eased back into his seat. I couldn't say what happened if I tried. It was one of those moments when things approached ugly, but pulled up short. Damien in his head thinking it wasn't worth fighting over, because he probably did feel like he was just playing and Droopy just making a point. He didn't know me, though. First person to stand up for me and in my head I was calling him an amigo, even if I never said it out loud. Latino dudes hate being called amigo. Standing in the pod, I felt bad about never learning the names of the two dudes who were always with him. Fairfax was the first place I'd talked to Latinos. I'd been painting them invisible the same way others had painted them. Throwing the same stereotypes at them in my head that I'd heard. Talking as if every Latino in America threw gang signs as a second language. It was ironic—I treated them the way I thought white people treated me, and I only began to think about it when Droopy stepped up to stop a bully from picking on me.

I adopted a language. Said "co-defendant" instead of Brandon, and made my words sound as coarse as what I heard from the deputies and inmates around me. *Inmates*, another one of those words that entered my vocabulary with the clank of steel and shouts of men missing the way their feet felt in a pair of Timbs. But I didn't say *amigo*. I never corrected anyone else, but let the word stay off my lips after I got into the adult block. When I heard brothers say it at the spades table, or walking down the hallways from visits or for whatever reasons they said it, it always sounded like the way some white men could make *nigger* a reason to fight. Droopy and the two Latino cats he hung out with rarely talked to anyone. Droopy talked, I think because he'd been locked up for a minute. The other two kicked it with each other. It was easy for them to do that. They were the only ones who spoke Spanish, and the one from New York, who said he was a Latin King, had a deep "if I got the chance I'd cut your fucking throat" resentment toward niggas for calling him amigo.

7

The Meaning of a Tattoo

There were three Latinos in the block, one white man and six young black males. That was how it was in most every block in Fairfax, except for the ones dominated by Latinos. Droopy, three cells down from me, was from El Salvador. I would watch Droopy and his homeboys in the corner by the window and for a minute be just like everyone else in there, thinking all of them were Mexicans. None of them were from Mexico. I heard Droopy say, "This stupid muthafucka think every loco he see from Mexico." All of us must have been crazy in there, lucky, too, to make it through days without hurting each other. Two of them were from El Salvador and the little one from New York was born in Puerto Rico. My excuse for not knowing an El Salvadoran from a Mexican or a Puerto Rican was that I'd grown up in Suitland, an area as segregated as any place in the South in the sixties as far as my life was proof. Inner cities, and areas just a ways from inner cities, filled with nothing but black folks.

After what happened with Damien I started talking to Droopy on a regular. He told me about LA, about El Salvador. He taught me most of what I know about gangs in El Salvador and California. I didn't understand why young Latinos in El Salvador joined gangs if they knew the police would kill them in the street for wearing a tattoo that proclaimed affiliation. I didn't ask though, because half of the things I'd done to get me in prison didn't make sense. Droopy was the first person I'd known who was an illegal immigrant. The label didn't mean anything to me. It was another play on words, another add-on to my language. He was illegal in this country, but the pistol he pulled out on somebody meant he'd do some time here before getting deported. He would tell me stories of why folks came to America, the dream translated into food and opportunities in a way that I'd never thought about. After a felony those dreams vanished. It made me wonder, and stare at walls thinking about what a second chance meant to the guilty.

Most times folks didn't go into other people's cells. We went in our own cell and looked for peace. On a good night, though, if someone wanted to have a private conversation, or to just sit back and kick it without the reminder that you were locked up with a group of people you couldn't stand, you'd go into a cell and kick it. Droopy had his homies. He was in MS-13, a gang of mostly El Salvadorans that had a reputation for terrorizing parts of Virginia. Gang life seeped out of Droopy's pores. I can't think of him without thinking of the tattoos on his face, tattoos on his arms, tattoos on his shoulder blades. MS-13 everywhere. One morning guards took him out into the hallway and made him take off his shirt and spin around as they took pictures of his tattoos. It was as if they knew that the tattoos told a story to them that he wasn't willing to tell. His tattoos said he killed someone in '94. They said that he was an illegal immigrant from El Salvador and that if he was sent back there he would get murdered because of the tattoos. The tattoos announced he was a gangbanger. The morning Brandon and I were arrested, as we drove through D.C., there was a man in the middle of the street directing traffic with a brown paper bag in his hand. No one paid him any attention, except to scream curse words and honk their horns. The tattoos gave Droopy that man's authority, and still he wore them like he owned them, because he did.

One afternoon Droopy asked me to come into his cell and chill with his homies. It was me, the small Puerto Rican, Droopy and the kid who didn't speak English. After a minute, Droopy asked, "So why you in here." For a minute I thought he was asking me about my charges and I started to answer him.

"I carjacked—"

"Nah, homes, I mean why you in Virginia. I don't care 'bout your charges." No one had asked me why I was in Virginia before. I didn't have an answer for him. He may as well have asked me why I wasn't in school, or at home doing homework.

"Shit, I could say I don't know, but for real we came out here to rob somebody." The Puerto Rican whose name I didn't know started talking in Spanish. For a minute I caught what he was saying. *Loco, casa.* I heard words I recognized, but couldn't make them make sense. He told Droopy and the quiet kid a story in Spanish. For a minute the three of them looked at me like people must look at them when they struggle with English, not exactly like I didn't belong, but that they didn't feel like doing the work to make me understand. After a few minutes I told Droopy I was going to get on the phone. That's the moment I decided to learn Spanish. I wanted to be able to speak to Droopy and his folks in their language the same way they spoke to me in English, and I wanted to get rid of the expectation that they had to learn English and me, as an American, didn't have to learn anything. In school we'd spent years learning French, and after all those years of learning all I could say was *fermez la bouche*, French for shut up. I felt that I'd wasted time, and that high school had made the language about sitting in a class acting as if you'd learned something more than learning. I wanted to learn. I didn't even need to use the phone, just wanted to give them some space to speak without worrying about translating for me and me some space not to feel like an outsider.

8

Running from Trouble

No one asked. No one has ever asked, but if they did I would tell them. I ran from the police because I was guilty. We were in jail, and everyone was busy thinking of ways to get out of what they'd done. Too busy to be asking for jailhouse confessions. Another juvenile got moved into the block with me after a few months. JR. He was a big young boy. Taller than me by a head with skin a shade off of mine. He got eleven years and told everyone who listened that his co-defendant snitched on him. He told us like we could do something about it, like we would if we could. It made me think about what I would tell people about the morning I got locked up. My mother hadn't asked. I'd tell her though, I'd tell her I ran because I was guilty.

In my hands was the credit card of someone I didn't know and in my mind I was ending a sentence to my mother where I couldn't explain why or how I got into a jail cell. As I crossed the street cars shot past me without pause, and because the cop dropped back away from within arm's reach of my jacket, I thought I'd gotten away. He wasn't a cop anyway, just a Macy's security guard. We shouldn't have run. There was no avoiding looking guilty once our Timberland laces and the bottoms of our coats began to form a line parallel with the ground as we jetted through aisles and out the door. Brandon and I ran flush into wind and oncoming traffic. We strained to breathe thin December air that bargained against our escape.

That is one way to start this part of how my life became a derailed train. With a chase. Two black boys running as fast as they can from a decision they made. It fits together. And we were that, two black boys running as fast as we could. Away. Still, none of that says who we were a week before the crime had been committed. I wouldn't have had to tell my mother who we were. And once you begin explaining things to a judge you're already short. Police pursued us the morning of December 8, 1996. A Sunday morning. Brandon's mother was in church. I forget where my mother was, and only remember where his mother was because she always spent her Sunday mornings in church. It was a Sunday morning and we were in the mall buying arms and arms full of clothes. In eleven minutes we'd spent more money than I'd ever spent on anything. I know it was eleven minutes because I had a stolen cell phone and kept looking at it as if it were mine, and time was as precious then as it is now that I'm telling this story after getting caught, and pleading guilty, and spending nearly a third of my life in prison. Why should we have noticed the way store employees watched us, is what I'd say if someone had asked me. It was Sunday morning and the store was almost empty. Worse yet, we were breaking more than the law. We were breaking our own rule about not using someone else's credit card. On top of that, we'd exceeded the artificial spending limit set up just in case we were to, for some crazy reason, use another person's credit card. Somehow we'd heard that employees only called the manager if your total went past some magical number, and that part of the story makes us calculating and criminal. And that was the reason I ran harder than

I'd ever run in a suicide for basketball practice. I thought I was running away from my own suicide.

The faster we ran the farther we got away from Pentagon City. When I bent around the corner and under the bridge, I emptied my pockets of everything that wasn't mine. There was a driver's license with the face of a smiling white man staring back at me from a wallet. There may have been the picture of a woman in there. I threw it all in the dirt my heels kicked up. But I stopped; my chest was hurting. Brandon stopped, too. We had no idea where we were running, or what we were running toward.

The Pentagon is the headquarters for the Department of Defense. And in a one-month span in 1996 eight young black males were locked up on its grounds. Two different situations where young black males acted as if they didn't know there are more guns in those buildings than in some armories. The Pentagon is a small city of guns and any one of those guns is an excellent reason for people running from the police to avoid the place. My mother worked there, which was more of a reason for us to have avoided it. We didn't. The parking lot we ran into was nearly empty. I asked a man standing near a fence, "Where's the train station?" It was cold, and sweat dripped down my face. Brandon kept looking behind us. He told us straight ahead.

He lied. We ran right past the train station, past our one shot at freedom. We ran into the arms of twenty police officers. The guns pointed at my head made me think of every reason why I was wrong. The ground was cold, and when the cuffs went around my arms for the first time, they didn't fit.

One afternoon the deputies brought mail for me with my father's name on it. How he'd gotten my address I couldn't say. How he knew I was locked up I couldn't say. The news of cuffs clinking around wrists was somehow important enough for someone to tell him, as if after all those years of absence he could come on the scene and make it go away. My father wrote me a letter and told me he thought I'd been shot by the police. A week or so after I was arrested, some friends of mine stole a minivan from Pentagon City. When the police approached them at Pentagon City they didn't run, they drove off. They drove to the Pentagon because when you're afraid every direction that's not where you are looks safe. And like me, I'm sure they didn't realize where they were driving. When the police are behind you, every reason you shouldn't be where you are clouds your mind and you just move. I understand that now, understood it then. The police, though, after one van flipped over and the other stopped, surrounded them. From there the story is shaky. The only remaining fact I have is this: four of them were shot by the police.

Three or four days after it happened Paul came to Landmark. I knew Paul from around the way. He told me that the police just started shooting at the car that didn't flip over. Sam, Dashawn and John were in the van. If he was telling the truth, around forty shots got emptied into the van, but I don't know any more now if he was telling the truth about the number of bullets than I did then. I knew the bullets were true. The charges got dismissed because of all the blood that spilled when the boys didn't have a gun. John and Dashawn were in intensive care. My father's letter said he thought I was one of the boys in the van, and that was half of the reason he started looking for me, wondering where I was and if I was okay. I was only half okay, not shot up but still locked up facing more time than he'd lived on the earth. In the letter he didn't ask me for an explanation, which was good, because I didn't have any.

The morning we got arrested the sun was out. The police said that we were too young to be taken to the jail. At first, because he's so tall, the cops didn't believe Brandon was fifteen. We walked into the jail in handcuffs. There were steps, and then we were split up. A balding officer, with the same belly that kept the cops on TV from ever catching the criminals in a foot race, led me to a bare room. It was the kind of room cops take you to when they plan on beating on you. The only pieces of furniture were a small desk and two chairs. The room was musty and warm, but I shivered as the officer cuffed me to the table. Then he walked out. The walls were a shade of white. The table metal. My heart was a frog trapped in my fist. What did I know about lawyers? This was my first time arrested, my first time talking to a police officer. I wanted to talk to the police officer. I thought there was an explanation for a license that didn't belong to me but had my fingerprints all over it in a patch of dirt under a bridge that I didn't know the name of. Why wouldn't I have thought I could talk my way out of it? Why wouldn't I have been ready to say anything to get out of the room that was musty and hot and leaving me shook?

What I learned is that Miranda rights mean nothing when you don't understand what it means to talk with the police. When the officer starting explaining my right to remain silent and that anything I said could and would be used against me, how was I to know that my silence couldn't be used against me in court? Why would I have been thinking about that when I was trying to figure out how I'd gotten the cuffs around my wrists? The police wanted to lock me up and they wanted to get me to confess to committing a crime. I didn't understand that; I thought there was a gray area where it became about resolving the situation the best possible way. When the potbellied cop walked into the room with the tape recorder, I didn't get nervous. He didn't *ask* if he could tape our conversation; he simply said he was going to tape it. He knew the fact that I ran made me guilty of something. So why would Miranda rights mean anything to him? He never asked me if I needed to call someone and I never asked to call anyone. In short, I confessed without my blood being splattered into the corner of that room. I was just negotiating with the police. I told him I knew a little something. I left Brandon out of it. This is what I'd brag about: I told on myself but not on him. I never asked what he told the police. Why did it matter anyway? I was guilty and had told them that much, and when I told them that much, it was just like I told them Brandon was guilty, too. I didn't know that then, but he ran with me and that running implied a guilt I doubt he could have shaken even if he hadn't pled guilty. He ran with me. I didn't know what Miranda rights meant, and didn't know that every time you open your mouth in a room with the police, there is a judge somewhere replaying the incidents of the crime in his head to determine the sentence of someone just like you.

FIRST DAYS

Even after my confession I thought I was going home. They didn't drive me home. They drove me to Landmark Detention Center, a juvenile detention center in Arlington, Virginia. "Detention center" is a euphemism, a movement away from "juvenile hall" or "reformatory." Landmark was new. Employees manning computers controlled the cell doors and doors to the outside. The first room I walked into was a large holding cell. I stayed in there for a few hours, pacing every inch of the room.

I didn't think about all the work being done on my case already. I had no idea about police reports being filed and intake reports. My confession was probably being entered into the public record, while some police officer told another about what's wrong with young people. I suspect, at some point, my victim was contacted. It even sounds wrong writing it: my victim. As if I owned him then and still own him. Our lives tied by an invisible rope we call felonies.

I did a number of things that first day, although many of the memories have been erased by other first days. The police arrested, fingerprinted, photographed and interrogated me after laying me on the ground under the watch of aimed pistols and showing me the inside of a paddy wagon for the first time. After being processed, the police learned I was sixteen; my age, an afterthought, brought up in the midst of Miranda warnings and a piecemeal confession. Still, my age was the key to my going to the juvenile detention center instead of the county jail I'd been moments away from being taken to.

Once I was finally out of the holding cell, the detention center staff took me to a room where my clothes were swapped out for their uniform. My blue jeans, T-shirt, Timberlands, socks and underwear were all exchanged for a dingy yellow T-shirt, a pair of sweatpants that barely fit and a secondhand pair of boxers. I'd never worn anyone else's clothes before, but any objection I had got wedged in my throat and wouldn't be heard. I remembered, years ago, my aunt had a huge bag of clothes from the Salvation Army and I thought it crazy to wear something someone else had worn, especially underwear. For shoes they gave me a pair of blue slip-ons made by Bob Barker. They looked like skateboard shoes and reminded me how far away from there I wanted to get. Had you asked me a month before that day, December 8, 1996, where I wanted to be, without question I would have told you Georgia Tech. I wanted to play point guard and get a degree in engineering. I would have told you how I'd run for class treasurer so that I could throw it on my résumé, and that I was looking into hooking up with a black engineers' association through the man who called himself my mentor. I would have told you that smoking weed was just something I did to pass the time.

I still hadn't talked to my mother and asked the staff taking me to my cell for a phone call. Real life had made the idea of one guaranteed call and talking to your lawyer a fantasy, but any indiscretions on the part of the police would get glossed over because I had admitted guilt, and in the end rules are for the innocent. The detention center limited phone calls to five minutes. I was accustomed to making phone calls that stretched into the night and ended with me asleep, the phone on the pillow beside me, some young girl asleep on the other end. The idea of telling my mother that I was locked up left me with chills. And because I could think of no one else to call, no other person who would begin to feel this deep blow I'd dealt myself, no one who would have that real a stake in getting me out, I called; waited maybe two rings before her tired voice answered and began the ordeal that defined my young life.

"Boy, where are you?"

"Ah, Ma, I'm in jail . . . it's a misunderstanding . . . ah . . ."

"What, for what . . ."

"I didn't do it. A car, stolen, me, a friend, ah, hard to explain . . ."

The reality of my situation sank in when I told my mother that tonight I could not, at one, two or even twelve in the morning go and get her a glass of water. Then, too, the pain of the stupidity of it all was there, as I tried to explain, and began to lie when the explanations turned to dust in my mouth.

This was the first time I lied to my mother about anything of consequence, and ironically, as the weight of what I said dawned on me, I realized the five minutes were far more than I needed. I retreated into a weak, "Ma, I got to get off the phone." How could I know then that the crime—a carjacking and a robbery—would make the news? How could I know that only that morning a friend had tried to call and tell me how the crime I'd decided to commit made the news the morning after it was committed? The lies fell flat to my mother's ears as lies as soon as I spoke them.

If someone asked me about the morning I was arrested, I would tell them that story. JR was in the block with me and his story was different. His story was filled with a co-defendant who snitched on him. Having someone tell on you makes your story different, means that on the first level you don't have to deal with the wrongness of the crime because you have to deal with the wrongness of being snitched on. In retrospect, I'm glad I told on myself, that I walked into the jail without knowing how to deal with the cops and confessed before I knew what was going on. The potbelly probably thought I was naive and smiled to himself as he typed up the paperwork. He might have thought that, but I know had the judge looked at the circumstances around the case, had anyone looked at the circumstances, from the very first moment they would have noticed that I wasn't hardened, just a kid who'd gotten himself into more trouble than he could handle.

9

The Tale of a High School Diploma

T he light from the sun moved through the window and shined on the metal of the picnic table. A group of men were staring at the television. The newscaster reported that Biggie Smalls had gotten shot up in his truck. The last music in the car I drove to a fistful of felonies was Pac's *Makaveli*. If anyone in the block was listening to me, I would have told them that I was in the eleventh grade when Tupac got killed. That I'd literally skipped the twelfth grade and finished high school from the inside of a jail cell. Suitland High School wasn't written across the top of the diploma, although I'd spent three years there. The diploma wasn't issued by the Maryland Board of Education. Getting certified as an adult meant getting transferred to the Fairfax County Jail, and that meant that no matter how things shook out, high school diploma or GED, it would be issued by the Virginia Public School system. If I had slanted the piece of paper I held in my hands that day against the light in just the right way, the fluorescent bulbs would make the letters unintelligible and let me imagine the paper was anything I wanted it to be. I would have imagined the paper was a notice of early release.

I heard someone say, "Damn, you see that shit." It was a question and a statement. Pictures of the truck Big was in when he got shot flashed on the screen.

I said, "Ay, y'all remember *Ready to Die*?" It came out when I was in the ninth grade. I hadn't smoked a blunt yet, and hadn't seen my father since I could remember. Everyone remembered the album. "When the joint came out I had just come home." This is what Joe says. In all his stories he'd just come home, just got locked up or was doing something that could get him locked up.

No one said that we were all locked up because of what filled the lyrics of rap songs. I didn't say it either. I thought about it sometimes, when the radio was on and I nodded to somebody rapping about who they were going to shoot and when. I didn't think about it the morning I walked into the block and no one said anything about the blue padded envelope in my hands that held my high school diploma. I was sixteen the morning Ms. Elman handed me that envelope. She was the reason I got the diploma. During my first week in the adult population I'd gone to her GED class looking to enroll in school. I spent fifty minutes in her class that first day. Every chair in the room had a body in it, black men nearly spilling into the hallway. For many of them school was nothing more than a chance to get outside the cellblock, walk down the halls and hope to catch a look at the women prisoners who walked the hallways with us but were locked up on the other side of the jail.

After the class I went up to speak with her. "How old are you?" she asked. She was a small middle-aged white woman and I couldn't imagine she'd care about my age. I was thinking about how easy I thought the math on the board was and that I'd learned it in middle school. How to add and subtract fractions. I told her I was sixteen. I looked at the room now that it was mostly empty. Theoretically the GED would lower recidivism rates, give people an opportunity to earn money as they increased their level of education. I doubted that it worked that way. The few people in the block who took the program seriously only did so to the degree that it took to pass the test, but it wasn't likely that the job you'd get with a GED would be that much better than the job you'd get without one if you were still barely literate. People were motivated to attend school because everyone thought school was something the judge took time off for, like good behavior. Most people anyway. There were always a few people dedicated to learning. When I met Ms. Elman I didn't want to get my GED, but I wanted time off of my sentence for as many things within the jail that I could be involved in. And I wanted more books to read. The classroom was smallish, without a chalkboard, and littered with tattered GED prep books. A small desk off to the side looked unused and made me realize Ms. Elman had stood for the entire class.

Maybe I reminded her of her son. She wanted to know what school I'd attended before I came to the jail and what classes I'd been taking. "Pre-calculus, physics, honors English, AP U.S. history, French 4 and computer math," I bragged because she listened to me as if it was important that I'd been taking physics. She hadn't asked my charges yet. And within a week she had enrolled me in some alternative school and I became one of the first two people to receive a high school diploma while locked up in Fairfax County Jail.

Often at the jail I felt I was there and not there. I saw the news, I heard the people arguing about whatever they argued about. But for minutes at a time I could sink into my world. Although I wrote letters every week I didn't tell anyone all the books I read, the nights I spent writing in a journal to make sense of the books and the cell I was in. Every day I walked down the hallways of the jail to the classrooms. The hallways are the most well-lit places in the building. Huge windows let sun into the wide areas, almost as if the deputies and inmates both needed more strength as they returned to the dimly lit pods and offices.

In the pods, men found as many ways to do push-ups as there are fingers on two hands. There were incline push-ups, decline push-ups, push-ups standing on your head, wheelbarrow push-ups, diamond push-ups, wide, close-in, a walking ten, a walking twenty and on and on until somehow a man pushed his way through his bid. We did push-ups to drain our muscles of energy, to clear our heads and maybe make time move more quickly toward what we all hoped for—a suspended sentence.

Ms. Elman was an English teacher by trade and she made it easier for me to beat the time back. I worked harder in English for her than I'd ever had to in high school. Before I'd gotten in trouble we were reading *The Scarlet Letter.* I wondered if there was a letter for this. If there was an *F,* for felon, that would go on my chest when I was released, or if I would be branded on the forehead with a *J,* for juvenile, so everyone would know my age when they saw me doing laps around the prison rec yard. *The Scarlet Letter* was the first novel an English class in Suitland High School had required us to read. Ms. Elman assigned maybe three books a week. I read *Sophie's Choice,* a book about King Arthur and his knights, Baldwin's *Giovanni's Room* and *The Catcher in the Rye.*

We had an agreement. Since I was already reading so much, Ms. Elman let me read whatever I wanted. She'd even order books for me, but if I read the book I had to write a response piece about it. Then, too, my mother could bring me books, as long as I read them for school. The reading gave peace to all the time I spent awaiting my sentence. I was in jail the first time I read a book cover to cover without stopping. *A Lesson Before Dying* by Ernest J. Gaines. The book was about a young teacher's relationship with a boy who'd been sentenced to death row for a murder he didn't commit. He'd walked into a store right after two men had robbed the place and killed the owner. The teacher mentoring him and the young boy were both black and the point of the mentoring was for the boy to walk to the electric chair knowing he was a man, not a pig and not a killer. There was a point at night, lockdown, when the bright lights were shut off. All that was left was the dampened glow that comes with incarceration. The dull night-light that will never go off, that makes you both prisoner and child. That's where I began to understand something about what Gaines was saying about humanity. I read under that light, and didn't stop reading until breakfast was served and I'd read the last page. I thought about what the death penalty meant, and what it meant to go to it as a man, especially for a crime you didn't commit. I was guilty and barely holding up.

The first time my mother saw my diploma, we stared at each other through a quarter-inch-thick slab of Plexiglas. Each of us held a telephone to our ear, and I pressed the diploma against the glass. My mother cried when she saw the slip of paper tucked inside the navy blue portfolio. I was sixteen when I received the diploma. People were surprised to see pictures of me posing in a burgundy graduation gown against a whitewashed brick wall. Friends wanted to know when they began holding graduation ceremonies in jail. Seeing me in a cap and gown was so surprising that no one asked where the other graduates were and I didn't tell them that the paper rolled, like a diploma, in my hand was a slip that gave me permission to be outside of my cell. If you didn't stare at the picture too hard, it looked just like a graduation picture, and people could imagine I'd just walked off the stage, exhilarated. People could imagine I was triumphantly on my way out of my mother's house. They didn't have to think about how cold it got the winter of 1996 like I did, and how the spring of 1997 didn't get any warmer inside the cell I lived in, shut away from family. I'd already walked away from my mother's house.

My high school diploma was tied to the conversation about Big, and Big was tied to Tupac. The afternoon we found out Big had been shot the old head wouldn't stop talking. "You know, rap music why half y'all young niggas locked up." He was ready to break out into some Curtis Mayfield or Marvin Gaye, anything he thought would cure us of a fascination with the music that he said ushered us into jail cells and graves. There never were many older men in the jail with me, and the few there usually felt the way he did, blaming baggy jeans, black-on-black crime and the rise in the incarceration rate on hip-hop. Part of me agreed with him, remembered the track on *Ready to Die*, where Biggie ruthlessly rapped about carjacking a pregnant woman, but I also knew that the music hit more notes than just those.

"Why you in here then?" I didn't hear who said it, but it bounced off the old head's ears. "Why you in here?"

The old man kinda smiled his gap-toothed grin before he said, "Nah, blood, you ain't gotta worry 'bout me. I'm 'bout done living. You gots to find out why you in here."

Two weeks later the old head's words were still in my head. K., a young dude just two years older than me, had moved into my cell. In conversation we figured out that he knew my younger sisters and lived around their neighborhood until his arrest a couple of months before he was to graduate from high school. It was crazy that neither one of us lived in Virginia. Wild, too, because it took just three days to be able to say I'd spent more time with him than I'd spent with my sisters in their lives. My sisters and I share a father, but I'd gone years and years without seeing him. Long enough for him to make another family. I was fifteen years old and staring into my sisters' faces for the first time and my father's face for the first time that I could remember. I realized that within the small space of jail and jail cells my life was resurfacing. It made me wonder why I heard Tupac talking about juveniles getting sent to prison with adults on "Shorty Wanna Be a Thug" and "Life Goes On," but never for a second thought it could happen to me, even as I walked into the night with a pistol in my hand. And it made me wonder what my father and sisters thought when they found out I was locked up. I knew what my mother thought, what her sisters thought.

Running into my past that way made me think of how K. and I arranged our lives into testaments that seemed to prove the negative stereotypes true. Two black teenagers in a cell together, both facing over forty years in prison, would seem to make that true. Except the jail cell, the charges we faced, even the anger that surfaced when we talked at night were just details that made it easy for people to shine a light in our faces and put us on a stage to play some designated role. We both figured that if we were two white teenagers with the same charges we'd be at home. In retrospect, we might have been wrong, but I know everything about my crime and life screamed aberration to anyone listening. K. would have been at home because I knew his crime. How he and a friend were rolling around and jumped out a car on two white boys. K. said he punched one of the dudes in the face and then took the money out his pocket. It was around five dollars, change included. He took the other boy's fake gold watch. His thirty seconds amounted to two robbery charges. I asked K., "You think about the dudes you robbed?"

He didn't say anything. We'd found ourselves in a place where people didn't think too much about victims. There wasn't enough room in that small cell for understanding when we both faced more time than we'd lived combined. No one would admit they deserved forty years for punching someone in the face. There was a spades game being played for our lives and our opponents had set the deck. We'd helped them. K. punched the boy in his face, took a watch and some change; I pulled a gun on a man asleep in his car. And maybe we should have been thinking about our victims instead of our anger, thought about them more than we thought about how cold a cell can get no matter the weather. The old head wanted to blame it on rap music, and often we wanted to blame it on racism, on the society that birthed us or on the streets that gave us the language of violence. The blame didn't work. It made me more alone, and kept me from thinking about how my sisters, wanting a brother, had to write him in a jail cell because I decided the weight of a gun in my palm gave weight to my voice.

I knew when I went before the judge he'd talk to me like I didn't think about the victim. He'd act like I didn't remember knocking on the driver's-side window asking him if he were a cop. The man was surprised by the question, but I was thinking about the man who'd gotten shot when he'd tried to carjack a man at some mall a few weeks before I walked up on the man sleeping in his car. I couldn't shake it from my head as I walked to the car. I knew I wouldn't tell the judge this, it said I was calculating and a fool. And it's not much worse than that. He wouldn't believe the gun didn't make me feel invincible, but trapped. I asked K. what he thought about his victim because I was thinking of what I'd say. I brought my victim into the room with me at night for a long time. He sat on my bed and stared at me.

He sat beside my mother and my little sisters. My family wanted me to care about something besides the way it feels to push up against a door and know you can't open it, and I couldn't. I would talk to the victim in my head, explain that he wasn't hurt, that he was taking it to extremes. I said that all I did was throw some bullshit ass CDs out of his window. I told the victim as scary as the idea of being in prison is, the cell door not opening when you want was scarier. I told him the cell not opening was like having someone wake you from your sleep with a pistol every night. I was afraid I'd go to prison and have something terrible happen to me and then have the world tell me that's what I deserved.

All of it taught me that I was by myself in the cell. Even when I had a cell partner, I was alone with my thoughts. I'd never told my mom this, never told any of my friends. I stopped talking to most of my friends the day the cops clamped cuffs around my wrists, and as I write this I know the story is about cuffs as much as it is about anything else. I got letters. Bags of them in the months I spent at the jail, but they all were a one-way conversation. People told me about what went on in their lives and expressed concern about me—I said as little as I could with as many words as possible. I taught myself the secret of survival: learning to do it all alone.

10

Joseph's Hand

One moment you could be the quiet person who sits in the corner minding your own business, and the next you can be someone's idea of a victim. Not in the systematic, everybody-who-goes-to-jail-gets-tested way that is described in most conversations about jail, but by the luck of the draw. You run into the wrong person on the wrong day, you get put in the wrong cell. As the faces in the blocks I found myself in changed, and the faces within those blocks changed, I began to understand something about how life in prison worked. There was a kid there named Joseph. Quiet. He would sit at the metal picnic table near the back of the pod. The table was right under the window, but we were so far away from the streets it didn't seem like just the third floor. One day I asked him, "What's that you're drawing? And why you holding the pen like that?"

"It's how I learned it. Instead of trying to make everything with straight lines, I use scratches."

The paper under his arms was filled with small fine scratches. I'd never seen anyone draw like this. Joseph was weird in his quiet way, so I halfway expected it. "Man, who draws with scratches? It doesn't make sense. But damn, that does look like a real hand. Where'd you learn to draw that way? Was it school?"

He looked at me sideways. His head still tilted down toward the table and his eyes squinted. "Nah, man, some of it I got from school, technique and whatnot, but most of it was my style before."

Joseph was drawing a man. The pen was parallel with the table, almost lying against the paper. At home, the McDonald's had just taken the first batch of hot fries out of the oil and in my mind I searched for the name of my fourth-period teacher. Physics or pre-calculus, but definitely a class I wouldn't make as I watched Joseph draw. Truth is, even a few months before I got myself locked up, I'd stopped going to math because my teacher was on maternity leave and I'd stopped going to physics because I knew I'd already earned a B without having to show up for the last week. Watching Joseph draw in that tiny cellblock where ten men tried to stay out of each other's way made it obvious how far away from school I'd come. There was a man who slept in the corner cell who was so silent I never learned his name. He didn't argue about anything, didn't rush to the slot when they passed out sandwiches for lunch, and didn't complain if no one passed him one. He wasn't scared, more lost in whatever night landed him in that corner cell.

I went to prison and found creativity I'd never thought to search for on the streets. I hadn't been there for a few months and ran into Joseph, drawing in a way that broke down all my ideas of what a picture should look like and what it should do. I never saw anyone draw with an ink pen in their hand like a Newport. When I looked over his shoulder, I saw the start of a hand. I had to remind myself that he was only using scratches. It was crazy; the hand flashed before the outline of what Joseph said would be a face. There was already fear there—his self-portrait. Joseph was older than me by two years, maybe, but skinnier and younger. Younger because he walked unsure of whether his next step would be in prison or home. People sensed that. He couldn't even talk tough.

You could forget Joseph if you tried. And it was weird because you could be almost invisible to some, and then have some people think or act like you're all they can see, buzzards that wanted to light on a weak man's back if given the opportunity. That's why it didn't matter that his art was brilliant. And that's why the picture he was drawing looked just like him: afraid. It was a symbol for the idea that art can translate, subconsciously and consciously, your world into your images. I was looking for the thing to immerse myself in so the world would recede, the way his eyes lost the rest of this scene when he'd scratch out his drawings. Maybe I wanted that moment he had, but I wanted it without the fear that was with him the rest of the time. In a way I made Joseph my case study. Let him be the guinea pig I watched try to adapt to the new environment.

Whatever his talent, Joseph and his picture did no more than circle the periphery of my life then. Afternoons were still dominated with the thought of court and all the little things that went with it. For months and months I had no physical contact with people who weren't locked up or guarding people locked up, unless I had a visit from my lawyer or some other state employee. Those visits were always contact. One afternoon I'd just come back in the block from a meeting with my lawyer, Emmanuel Lowery. He was a large man, and told me he'd gotten strong doing farmwork. And this is the thing: he was black. We joked about my first lawyer, a white man who told me he was better than Cochran, who told me that I'd spend a year in jail at the most. I wasn't but sixteen but knew a lie, and fired the attorney with the name I can't remember. Lowery was different, black and straight up with me. "The gun means a mandatory three-year minimum." He told me he'd do a sentencing memorandum to argue that the mandatory minimum could still be suspended because I was a juvenile. Mr. Lowery sat with me in a small cramped office, one of several along a hall with one door that had glass you could see through. In every one of the rooms a man with an inmate tried to figure out when he'd be free, and in a way, what will devastate me for the rest of my life is that I began thinking about my future as a tangible thing only after my life teetered on the hope of a brief.

I knew black lawyers existed. I could tell you about Thurgood Marshall. And so this story isn't about the black boy who had no idea of what he could become until he found his life dominated by the professional folks, black and white, who dominated the legal system. But having a black lawyer meant that I wanted him to understand I wasn't a menace to society. It meant moving from the nonchalance and arrogance that dominated how I looked at the court proceedings. I understood how it looked on paper, how the night I carried around a pistol looking for a victim inspired anyone with good sense to disbelieve everything I said. So I gave him the essays I'd been writing, told him more than he needed to know to work my case, and was happy that he listened. In return, he gave me this compliment: he said he wished he'd met me before the mess of robberies and pistols began. I always thought of it as just one crime, but he reminded me that I faced a carjacking, attempting carjacking, robbery, attempted robbery and two use of a firearm in the commission of a felony—charges all stemming from one night of madness. The tragedy was that I could have navigated the little bit of violence and drugs that I grew up around, but would have done it without having any real chance of speaking to a black lawyer, white lawyer or any other professional outside of the teachers I saw every day. While I talked to Mr. Lowery, I knew that my defense was that I was young, gifted and black with no guidance. And I knew that wasn't an excuse for carjacking.

walked into the block after talking with my lawyer with my head down. When I looked up I saw Joseph at the table again. The table became an extension of him. Damien asked, "What's Joseph doing?" He knew what he was doing, sitting down at the table making scratch marks on a sheet of paper, but he didn't know what that amounted to.

"He's drawing. Scratches and crooked lines, but it comes out to something you recognize. Right now, though, I don't know what it is."

"How you know he's drawing then?"

Everyone else was waiting on soap operas, but Damien didn't watch them. He was one of the people around the TV every afternoon at four for *X-Men* and *Tom and Jerry Kids*. It was crazy that the jail reduced grown men to watching kid shows for entertainment, as if we were all still little youngins waiting for the Saturday morning cartoons.

"I don't know how I know he's drawing, besides the fact he told me. How else I'm gonna know he drawing. Right now the shit don't look like nothing. It's just a bunch of scratches, but a bunch of scratches is how he does it. You got to look at it though. It looks like a hand."

"Shit, if I could draw like that I wouldn't be in this jail."

I wondered how he knew he wouldn't be in jail if he could draw. I remembered Joseph telling me how he got into a school but couldn't go because he didn't have the money. What do you do when you have a skill and no way to further it, no way to put yourself around the people who can show you how to turn your skill into money for rent or a car note or a mortgage? Damien needed to make himself different from Joseph, because to walk into a jail cell without skills meant there was a chance you could redeem yourself through something you'd learn to do with your hands. And if nothing else, it meant that you had an excuse. You robbed the man because there weren't any jobs for people who didn't graduate from college that paid more than minimum wage.

Joseph stopped drawing. He listened to us, he saw us watching him. He didn't want the attention. His hand shook, or maybe it was just me thinking that he knew what we were thinking. I didn't know. I couldn't draw. There was a man in the block with us named Tim. He couldn't draw either. Tim acted like he thought Joseph was his little brother, but I think Joseph knew better. In his thirties, Tim had already done a bid down at Greensville, the prison he bragged about like it was attending Yale. A *bid* was nothing more than a stretch of time a man called a cell home, and with Tim it was always the Ville this and the Ville that, as if his doing time gave him entrance into an exclusive fraternity and not the five years' worth of memories of life in the state penitentiary. Tim messed with Joseph in the pod, but I swear he was just finding excuses to touch him. And the way Joseph looked at him said he knew, too. The hand he drew covering that face was probably his hand. It reminded me that when you're in a fight and you know an arm is coming at you, and you don't know what else to do, you throw an open hand before your face to block it, or catch the punch. The whole while looking away, wishing you could be somewhere else, wishing you could be somebody else. I think that's what Joseph was saying with the picture. He had that hand up first and the eyes looking away because those were the most important things. He knew things were coming that he couldn't dodge.

Joseph finished his picture early one morning. It had taken him twenty-six days, or the span of seventy-eight meals pushed through the slot doors. He drew with a black pen. The arm in the picture extended as if it was reaching out to touch your face. At first that was all you noticed. All the strength left in Joseph's world was in that arm. He'd given it size, cords of muscles made out of the same swirling marks that made the hand so real. The arm extended only to give you the hand. It pushed away from the face, toward the page forming almost a perfect right angle. There was no shoulder the arm connected to; it shot up from below the margin at the bottom of the page. The forearm had seen heavy lifting.

The arm presented the hand. That right hand with fingers splayed wide. For a moment, when I looked at it the first time, I thought the hand was life-sized. There were thick calluses on the index and middle finger. I didn't know how Joseph got three dimensions on a sheet of paper, but those calluses made that hand a workingman's hand. It made me think about the jackhammers and construction equipment we heard throughout the day. Men outside were building a bigger, newer jail. Joseph was building the world of a man locked in an old, small jail. The scratches became whorls, and I could imagine all the lines were just another prison that I wanted to crawl out of. And the extended hand Joseph drew, the fingerprints on that hand, were all that was left to protect the scared face.

11

Another Bullet to the Brain

t was earlier than early. The raggedy-mouth trustee who pushed carts of metal trays carrying our breakfast down the hall each morning was still asleep in his bed somewhere; the cooks who fixed up the pancakes and eggs were probably just getting up, sleep still in their eyes. It was May 16, 1997. My sentencing day. The deputies hadn't opened my cell door yet, but I was up. Staring into the half darkness of a cell with a night-light thinking about what would happen in a few hours. My cell partner was in his bed, asleep, not thinking about my fate and honestly I know I wasn't thinking about him. I could have been thinking about Terrence Johnson that morning. Terrence Johnson, go-hard or infamous, depending on who's telling the story, cop killer who got off easy with a manslaughter charge or child hung out to dry by the racist justice system. Johnson wasn't but fifteen when it all happened: the age of my co-defendant; a year younger than I was when I sat in that cell. In 1978 he was tried as an adult and sent to prison for twenty-five years.

Where my aunt heard his name I couldn't tell you. She sang his praises, told me how he hadn't let being locked up get him down; how he'd earned his degree from a jail cell and was ready to go to law school. She left out part of the story—she didn't tell me that Howard University's Law School wouldn't let him in, not when all they could see was the blood on his hands. His story was supposed to tell me that I could make it out of the cells and into something better. And for a moment it did. But he'd killed himself in front of the bank he'd allegedly just robbed and the moment the bullet entered his brain made every test he aced and book he read meaningless.

When the door opened, I knew it was time to stop thinking about Terrence Johnson. I'd been dressed since the night before, so I walked out of the door with toothbrush and toothpaste in hand. I took my time brushing my teeth. I knew the toothbrush wasn't getting my braces cleaned the way they should be, but there wasn't anything for me to do about that. I walked back into my cell and jammed my feet into my sneakers as I dropped the toothbrush and toothpaste on my bed. "Betts, court in five minutes," a deputy called out as I walked back into the pod with a washcloth in my hand. The deputy looked surprised I was up and waiting for the door to crack open. That early in the morning, I could see out the window clearly. No one was on the streets in that new dawn light. Every day we heard jackhammers and the music of construction pounding below. I was stuck between two brick walls. On the other side of the window another jail was being built, and when I turned back into the block I had to face the rest of the day, and whatever sentence the judge decided to give me.

Deputy Jones took me to an A block on the first floor. The block is filled with people in protective custody. When I walked in there were five or six men cuffed and connected to a chain-link belt being led out of the block. The chain made all of their fates seem connected, and once they cuffed and locked me on it made me feel part of the forgiveness parade.

"What you gonna tell the judge when you get in there?" It's the first thing I heard when I walked into the block. Somebody yelled it out to someone else, and the answers ricocheted across the room.

"I'm a tell him I didn't do it, what the fuck you think?"

"Man, shit, you told him that last time."

"I'm a start praying when he asks me to speak."

"Bet I tell that muthafuckin judge to kiss my ass."

The question had half the room chiming in on how to get around a prison sentence. It calmed me down as I waited to be led out of the room. The group of men in cuffs and chains were all ignoring the five or six deputies in the room, ignoring their chains, too, and in moments of laughter ignoring what standing in front of a judge meant. Maybe they'd been there before, I didn't know. But their moments of ease bolstered me, even as my group was ushered to an elevator. Six black faces on chains—and I knew this was going to be the theme of what was to follow if I didn't get released. Chains and black men.

I wanted to be invisible, so I didn't say anything. Even as they led us into a waiting cell and uncuffed us all I was quiet. We were the first group in and minutes later they brought another chain-linked belt of brothers in cuffs. All in all there were twelve of us in the holding cell that may have been comfortable for three. There was one toilet that already had the cell heavy with the smell of piss, no toilet paper. There was no room to walk around. The only bench ran along the wall with the toilet and there were five of us squeezed onto it. I'd crept onto the end of the bench closest to the bars up front and could see anyone coming or going. When the deputies walked away the room erupted in commentary. We were all going into courtroom F. I knew I had Judge Bach. In the moments before I walked into the courtroom I was surrounded by no less than eight jailhouse lawyers. Brothers who swore they could get anybody off of any-thing. Psychics, too, folks who could divine your sentence by the look on the faces of the folks returning.

We weren't together long enough to pass around names. So the nickname system was in place. I knew it when Matlock spoke up, "Young blood, what you in for?" This was sentencing day; guilt or innocence not one of the questions the judge was thinking about, so neither were we. "Carjacking." One word, just like that, "carjack-ing." I deadpanned it, too, 'cause you have to deadpan a crime that carries life. What did he say back to me? "I hope I don't go in there after you."

I marked the men by their attitude or crime and that's how they marked me. Matlock was Matlock 'cause he thought he knew every-thing. His system was pure. If the person who goes in before you gets *oiled up* you're going to get five, six more years than you would have otherwise. And if you were looking at probation, start looking at eighteen months. *Oiled up* was slang for getting a long sentence, one that seems disproportionate to the crime or to the way others have been sentenced. Matlock said to me, "If you was white, I'd give you a chance, but seeing as how the only white boy in here with us has a drug charge, you really out back."

Out back, as in hopeless, as in I shouldn't have been expecting to get less than seven years because my co-defendant had gotten seven years. *Out back*, as in there was a night I had a gun in my hand and I'd awakened a white man asleep in his car and the argument I made in my head about my age wasn't specious to me, but it was specious to Matlock who didn't even consider it in predicting that the over/under bet on how much time I'd get would be at twenty-five years.

There were bars on the front of the cell, the old school bars you expect to find in a prison cell. I gripped the bars and watched the people, one at a time, get escorted to court and come back in with their time. No one had more than a few years to do, most had less

than that. A few never came back, got time served and were released.
I thought about my lawyer, Mr. Lowery. After meeting me a couple
of times he taught me a word I'd never heard before. *Aberration.*
He said my crime was an aberration. All these years later and I still
remember the word, how it framed the way thirty seconds changed
my life forever but didn't have to define me. In John Edgar Wideman's
Sent for You Yesterday, Carl tells his nephew the story of Brother
playing the piano the first time. How Brother hadn't touched a piano
before Thursday but played so good on Saturday night that folks
thanked Jesus a day early. It didn't make sense to Carl that Brother,
his main man, more like each other's shadows than brothers, could
walk up to a piano and play it better than anyone in Homewood,
breath life in it. The way Carl felt about Brother and that piano was
the way my family felt about me and the night I ran around Virginia with a small automatic pistol tucked in my palm. It made them
not want to look at me straightaway 'cause it was no way I could
be the Dwayne they'd known since dirty diapers and spit bubbles.
Mr. Lowery, though, he had the word to explain it, *aberration.* My
robbing the white man and Brother at the piano both. Mr. Lowery
wanted the judge to understand that the gun was a onetime thing,
lightning striking, if you will. I figured it was like Brother playing
better than anyone in Homewood without warning, then quitting.

The problem was that once I got in the courtroom everyone had
to listen to the prosecutor's narrative. He hadn't spent sixty seconds
talking to me, but he thought he had me down. Said I was a chame-
leon who had everyone who loved him fooled. He argued that this
couldn't have been my first time, and that in one night I changed the
way an entire community looked at the holidays. The victim was in
the audience. He frowned when the prosecutor pointed to him and
nodded when the man called me a menace to society. The prosecutor
might as well have said I put a bullet in the man's brain the way he
talked about me. The management of the mall prepared a carefully

written letter that said I should be given the maximum punishment allowable by law as I was a threat to the safety of the community. As the prosecutor read the letter aloud, I wondered if the mall management knew that the maximum was a life sentence. I wondered if the prosecutor knew the maximum penalty was life.

12

The Forgiveness Parade

oes the defense have any witnesses to present to the court?"
Judge Bach asked from the bench. The courtroom was beautiful, dark wood everywhere. Since my guilt was established,
confessed to, there were only character witnesses to be called. Before
the judge were a few letters from my high school teachers, but what
can a teacher say to stack up against the "menace to society" rhetoric
of the prosecutor? I hadn't saved anyone's life to balance the one I'd
shattered, and I knew it. My family did, too, that's why their character witnessing amounted to one pitiful line that has been echoed
so often in courtrooms and sociology classes discussing the fate of
black boys that it burned my ears. Each witness walked to the witness stand and told the courtroom that I was a good boy without a
father. He hadn't been in my life so everyone thought it made sense
to hang my guilty plea around his neck, my guilty plea and the night
a gun was my false talisman. They needed to balance out the "menace
to society" speech the prosecutor gave. I knew this, but my mother
was in the audience, her voice stolen by a bout with bronchitis. At

least that's what the doctor said, but I knew a broken heart could make you stop talking. After the forgiveness parade went before the court and begged for my life, after they sat on the stand willing to fall on swords if it would keep me out of jail, the judge asked if I had anything to say. The most important day of my life and whatever I'd written for the past two weeks wasn't good enough a minute after I'd written it.

13

Penalties and Broken Illusions

y legs shake because that's what your legs do when you talk to a judge. My mouth, it's ready to open. I haven't thought for a minute about what to say. He doesn't want my life story. It's in the letter I wrote him. Behind me, the people want to finally know why I did it. I can imagine my aunt screaming in my ear, "Nigga, the fuck were you thinking about." But she's not screaming; she's sitting beside my mother and she's silent as a whispered prayer. I knew it was a bad thing to force my mother into this courtroom, bowing her head in prayer for me when there wasn't a thing that could save me from doing time. I could tell the judge that, but this isn't the time to try to rationalize. I should just cry, break down right here, except I don't have tears. Gotta be stone. First person in my family to stand before a judge like this, shackled and cuffed, begging for mercy. And this is all I got left right here, this moment to speak. After this, the judge is going to start talking, reading off words that signal if I leave out the door behind me or the one to my left. I've listened to everyone. Mr. Lowery has given the judge his sentencing memorandum. A well-put-together argument about how the judge had a greater leeway in sentencing me because I was a juvenile. And right now I have to think that the judge is ready to put his career on the line for me, to look the victim and the prosecutor in the face and say, "This boy deserves another chance." Truth is, if I was him, I probably wouldn't. Black boy I ain't seen from nowhere comes in my courtroom confessing to carjacking a man three weeks before Christmas. What kind of sympathy is that going to get me, especially when all the reason I have is a laundry list of family talking about how I didn't have a father. My mother quiet in the audience, half invisible. It's news to me that not having a father doomed me from the jump.

"Your Honor, I have to apologize to the victim. What I did was wrong. I apologize to my family, to my mother. But I have to say, your Honor, that I didn't do it because I didn't have a father in the house."

And after that everything is blank. My body light and ragged as if I've thrown myself on the mercy of the court for real, taking back the excuse handed to the court by my family and giving no answer in return. What answer does the court want, does anyone want? That I didn't really give a fuck about the victim, that I thought the crime was something of the moment that wouldn't define the rest of my life? My legs still shake, wobble like a fighter who's ready to fall.

Once I told my mother she should be happy that all I did was get suspended from school, suspended for a stink bomb. I told her at least I wasn't like Malcolm X, who had to go to prison to become what he'd become. Your mouth will get you in trouble. I thought it was funny then, when crime just wasn't in the realm of possibility to me. Two years, though, will change a lot. I should have told the judge that, how in two years crime went from unfathomable to regular. Not right, but regular: something in the realm of everyday possibility, something more real than the college degree I figured I'd get. The judge wants a reason that will make it okay for him to send me home, when the only reason is some boys are willing to walk further out on the ice than others, and everyone has their own reasons, but mostly it's just because they're boys and they think they can, they think they can and are more afraid to not walk out on the ice than to risk falling in the water that will definitely kill them. I stepped out there once. Just one time is what I tell the judge. The gun in my hand was the first. Never even fired the thing. It was on safety. It doesn't matter though, words aren't enough and this courtroom is all of a sudden as tight and claustrophobic as the shackles around my feet.

"I truly regret what has happened, your Honor, and hope to one day make amends."

In a courtroom a judge is expected to be many things, and even as a pencil-thin sixteen-year-old talking to one for the first time I knew candid wasn't one of them. Yet moments after I spoke the chief justice of the Fairfax Circuit Court of Virginia, the Honorable F. Bruce Bach told me, "I don't have any illusion that the penitentiary is going to help you, but you can get something out of it if you want to." Right there I should have known that I could cancel the next few Christmases.

Chief Justice Bach sentenced me to the minimum of fifteen years for carjacking, five years for robbery and a mandatory minimum of three years for use of a firearm in the commission of a felony. When he said that he would suspend nine of the fifteen years for carjacking and run the remaining six concurrent with the five years I had to do for the robbery, I still counted fourteen years. I didn't know what *concurrent* meant. The courtroom was stone silent as he read off the years I'd have to do in the state penitentiary. Once he finished talking, and the deputies began escorting me back to the holding cell, my auntie screamed. It sounded feral, and although I was shaking myself, I turned and yelled, "It's aiight. I'm cool." But I wasn't. I couldn't figure how I'd just gotten fourteen years in prison when I wasn't but sixteen years old. I had earned my high school diploma a year early, despite the trouble I was in. The teacher told the judge I was college-bound.

When I got in the holding cell I realized none of those things mattered. It was the gun, and the fact that there were no facts that made me appear salvageable to the prosecutor, to the judge, to the victim. He told me to my face prison wasn't going to help me and then sentenced every one of my one hundred twenty-six pounds to a cell for fourteen years. At least I thought it was fourteen years, until I learned that *concurrent* meant I'd serve two sentences at one time. A legal trick where the system would pretend that I was two people for my first five years: one, a sixteen-year-old black boy doing six years for carjacking; the other, a sixteen-year-old black boy doing five years for robbery. The whole time I'd be a stupid-ass nigga is what I thought, having put myself in a position to get burned by a system that burned black folks on a regular basis.

Once I got back into the cellblock, I laid my head on the table and listened to the radio. My teacher, Ms. Elman, came by and asked me how it went. Nine years, I said, and she shook her head. There weren't any words of encouragement to give. It didn't make any difference that I'd read lots of books, had a high grade point average or a high school diploma. I was no different from any other black male in a courtroom. In the block I listened to a couple of vicious jokes about how fucked up it would be in prison. Damien, Dred and Richard all going home thinking it was cool to try to scare the young dude. Droopy was already sentenced. He had five years and would be deported the day his sentence was up. K., who'd just punched a white boy in the face and taken a few dollars, had thirteen years. He wasn't but eighteen and could have taken a plea bargain for five years. I never did figure out why he chose to fight the case, but he did and got burned. Then there was Black. Black, who you couldn't forget was there because he was facing nearly as many life sentences as he had fingers. The rumor was he'd killed six people, and it had to be true, 'cause that was the only way you could stare that much time in the face. Point is, I didn't think about their time until I had to think about mine. And thinking about the time hurt.

TIME'S HEAVINESS

After I was sentenced, time was all I thought about. I was sixteen and headed to prison for nine years, which meant there would be no prom, no first night driving down Silver Hill Road, no going off to college. The time meant my life was different and would change in ways I couldn't imagine. I remember the first time after the sentencing my mother came to see me. The visiting room was still and when I walked in I might as well have been holding a clock with no hands. The phone in my mother's hand was scuffed and her knuckles strained against the black. But when she saw me she kissed her hand and placed it on the glass where my hand waited. What's more painful to a mother than to stare at her only son behind glass in a jail's visiting room? Around us the people talked about diapers, about appeals, about the deputy that split Twan's head open for nothing. I heard it, but it washed over me like the judge's voice passing down my sentence. I heard it all, but couldn't make out the sense of it and all the while I was drowning in the sounds. The face of the judge was in front of me. His face was behind my eyes. My mother was aging before me and her smiles were gone. She had come right after I was sentenced, right after the judge told the court he was under no illusion sending me to prison would help me.

"Mom, it's cool. I'm okay." But she was holding back tears, and she kept telling me that I was her only son. "Dwayne, you're my only son." I wanted it to be about what the judge had taken from me, from her. I wanted it to be about the time he'd given and how it was on my back even then, pushing me toward the ground. But my mom saw it different. When she said, "Dwayne, you're my only son," she was raising the question the judge didn't ask. If she cursed she would have asked, "What the fuck were you thinking?" And if I was brave or even honest I would have said, "Moms, I really don't know." But we were in a place where words didn't make the same sense anymore, and there was no room for questions when every moment was filled with anxiety about my safety. The green shirt I wore hung off my body. I told my mother that Lowery said there would be an appeal and I sounded just like the voices that were all around me, setting aside hope for another day. She didn't cry. She told me that everything was going to be okay. We didn't speak about God. We didn't speak about rehabilitation. I wouldn't say it aloud but at that moment God was another closing cell door. After hearing the judge sentence me I couldn't believe in anything but my own fear, and my own depression.

"Mom, it's just nine years. I can do nine years if I have to, but I'm sure I'll get it reduced on appeal." I talked to my mom as if I believed it, and maybe part of me did. The same way all of us who'd been found guilty thought we'd get out on appeal. I didn't know it then, but in all the years I was in prison, I never once saw anyone go home on appeal.

14

Transfer

Y ou're moved from the jail to prison when deputies tell you. People guessed, they speculated. But you didn't know until a deputy called your name over the intercom, told you to come to the booth and then passed you one of those industrial-sized black trash bags to pack your stuff. They gave you the big bag even if all you had to your name were the scrubs the county gave you to wear. Since my sentencing day I'd been waiting for the bus. Watched it drive into my dreams and bring me awake sweating. Seventeen now and I was still fearing prison because it was unknown and it made sense to be afraid of the inside of a cell. I gave away my radio. I dumped eight books, two bags of corn nuts, six brownies and all the letters I'd stacked up in over a year into a black trash bag without strings and sat it in front of the door leading to our cellblock. Among the books were Fanon's *Black Skin, White Masks* and a collection of W. E. B. Dubois's writing. The books had been the main thing keeping me attached to a dream of a future. I thought if I read enough and became smart enough, then I could prove I was somebody. I thought the books would somehow give me another shot at the world one day while letting me leave the world I was trapped in every day.

By the time of my sentencing there were few people left in the jail that I really talked to. Black was one of them, and he swore no one stayed there that long, not unless they were sentenced to less than eighteen months. I didn't believe him, but did when night came and I stared into my cell, empty of everything but me. You can't do nine years in a jail. Those nine months were rough. The rare times I'd gotten fresh air was out on the roof, surrounded by barbed wire and feeling the sun burning my back and face.

Now it was early Thursday morning and I hadn't slept. I'd been up most of the night and the tray slot still hadn't clanked signaling breakfast. The night before I stood on the edge of the empty bunk in my room. Black was beside me. "This Christmas you gonna be downstate somewhere. You lucky to be getting away from these red-neck muthafuckas." The court had given him three life sentences and the time left him praying he'd be away from the claustrophobia of the jail by Christmas. Every afternoon he was trying to talk it up. "I can't wait to get away from these racist muthafuckas." "You know you can get some pussy in the visiting room?" "For real, if commissary comes through here one more time giving us this list with nothing but Moon Pies and chocolate on it I'm a flip." It was always something different. A complaint hiding the pain that comes with doing something to earn yourself a life sentence. People who haven't been in prison don't know what a life sentence means, and even people in prison have a hard time understanding it. Back at Fairfax, Black couldn't understand it, couldn't wrap his arms around the clock with no hands the judge gave him. His pressing to get out of the jail was a need to stretch his legs out, to be able to move around more because maybe the space and a few more things on a commissary list would make things better.

I found out life in prison meant six hundred years in Virginia.

That it meant you live and die ten times before you can be a free man. I talked to Black because he could understand whatever time I had, and if I could understand how he dealt with the time he had without snapping, I knew I could deal with mine. The night before I left, Black was out of complaints. He was congratulating me as if I'd won something, and we were looking out of a window that stretches the span of my right arm and is as wide as my opened palm. It was late, not late enough for lockdown but late enough for the sun not to be out. We couldn't make out what was in the night if we wanted to, but I stared. We stared. For me, it was like staring into what was gonna happen when they shipped me. "When they shipped me" sounded like I was talking about myself as a box of oranges, and maybe I was.

"The food gonna be aiight," he said. I think he had something else to say. He let the sentence sit in the air for a minute and as I started to tell him the food might be fucked up, I realized he was already out of the cell. I wanted to tell somebody I was scared. Not Black though, you couldn't tell someone with a life sentence that you were scared. What couldn't be worse than knowing you have to spend the rest of your life in a cell like this?

I spent all night thinking about prison. I remember three weeks before I got shipped, two dudes in the block across from us had started fighting, and the tall light-skinned one hit his head on the corner of the table. Blood shot out from his head like a water hose with a hole in it. I didn't know him, but heard him all the time. Talking. Talking trash. I wasn't scared for him, but scared because I wasn't sure if I could have closed my fist and hit him so hard that his chin hit the table like that. A bunch of people at Fairfax were ready for prison. Black wanted my seat on the bus. I could understand that. Damien, Dred and some others, too, weren't going but seemed ready. Did I think they were ready because they were all grown, or simply because they said they were ready? Since many of them didn't

get sentenced to enough time to go down there, they could say whatever they wanted. I knew what I wanted. I wanted to go home, to
sleep in my own bed. But I didn't tell anyone that. The night before
I got transferred, people kept yelling up to my cell. I don't remember who said what, but I remember the chorus of shouts. "Dwayne,
young, my cousin down there, if you get sent to Nottoway look for
a light-skinned dude named Chris. They call him Spider though,"
I remember the voice yelling, and me thinking this is a fucked-up
place to have a family reunion.

"Betts, come on out." The voice of a deputy sounded over the
intercom. It was still early, and I'd been waiting for breakfast. I knew
that sometimes they moved you insanely early and other times you
left around lunch. I wanted every minute I could. All of a sudden jail
was safe and I didn't want to leave. My cell door creaked open. Last
night Black told me I shouldn't be worried. He said the same thing
about himself before he went to court, but he got three life sentences.
I realize now that Black and I looked at things differently. My steps
were taking me closer to home. I couldn't see that, but he could. He
knew that no matter where he moved there was no way to knock
down one life sentence, let alone three. I banged on his cell door.
"I'm gone, Black."

"Aiight, lil youngin, keep your head right." I think he told me he
was on the next bus out, but that didn't really mean shit. The same
way I was in the cell alone the night before, I knew I was going to
be alone for the bid. I heard other folks yelling. I woke someone up,
some folks were just up. *You gone now for real, huh? You should
have left me that food, you greedy-ass nigga. Don't take no shit. No
matter what get you a knife. On GP swing on the first nigga get you
wrong. Don't worry about it cuz, you gonna be aiight.* I heard it all
and didn't hear it. The cellblock door closed behind me; the deputy
led me to an elevator that took us to the first floor.

We sat down by the R cells for a good hour playing the waiting game. First we waited for them to bring us breakfast, and then we waited to find out what was going on. Black men of all ages lined the wall on either side of me. When you're the youngest, you always know it; nearly every face around me was covered with beards, mustaches or scowls. The oldest man approached sixty, his near-white beard what I'd expect to see on my father's father. He could have been him, and we could have been on that line together and I wouldn't have recognized his face. He wouldn't recognize mine either. His face looked hard, filled with nights of liquor and closed fists. He'd been there before, at least he moved with the ease of someone walking into a room they remembered. A line of black men with scowls on their faces. I wore my scowl, too; the one I adopted my first night in the cell. But I kept thinking mine was see-through. As if somehow I belonged there less than the men around me. But there was a stack of letters in my property bag, all from my father written from another jail somewhere.

I did what they do in the media: reduced the line of black men waiting to be sent to a prison in the southern part of Virginia to a stereotype. Thing was, everybody on that line was different. Their stories etched in the scars, smiles and scowls on their faces. I couldn't read those stories. Didn't know if they wrote their sons and nephews and cousins letters explaining manic-depression like my father did, or apologizing, or reiterating their innocence. I was in that line sizing up those men, deciding that they were whatever it was I'd heard about black men and prison, and by doing that I was sizing myself up. I was strapping on the albatross that reduced me to a number in a file.

I didn't know if the people around me were running the same

game on themselves. The youngin beside me had hair longer than my fingers. He didn't blink when the deputy told us both we were going to Southampton Receiving Center. "Damn, I wanted to go to the Ville," he said. The tooth in the middle of his mouth was cracked. The deputy walked past everyone with a clipboard in his hand calling out the names of prisons. Bland, Southampton, Greensville. I didn't know the difference, but noticed that only two of us were going to Southampton. The guy beside me and me.

Southampton. I spent half my young life running away from something only to find it one morning in Fairfax County Jail. Found a squad car to drive me to it. Prison. I always knew my father did some time, and I'd never wanted to be him. I should have said it out loud: I'm not going to be like my father. One minute I didn't know him, and the next, the only thing I knew for sure about him—that he'd been to prison—was also a fact of my life.

—

PART II

Running Toward the Past

No safety in numbers, like back on the block:
two's aplenty. three? definitely not.

—Etheridge Knight, "For Freckle-Faced Gerald"

15

A Different Kind of Road Trip

The car we got in was brown, a mirror image of the car that took me to the county jail, except this one announced that the Fairfax County Sheriff's Department owned it. A metal grill separated the front seats from where we sat. It was the kind of car somebody lived in, a shirt thrown on the floor between us, and the smell of too many days of fast food.

"Where you from, young?"

I turned my head to the left and looked at the young brother beside me. He sounded like someone I knew, talked with the same slang that I grew up with. "*Young.*" A language we shared, so I told him, "Maryland." The answer general as hell, a step forward and a step back because I didn't know why he was getting in my business and didn't think he'd know where Suitland was anyway. "Maryland," I told him again. "PG County."

"Oh yeah, I got folks out there. Out Forestville. You know that McDonald's over there by the mall? My aunt used to live out there."

As the car moved slowly out of Fairfax, it was like seeing the place for the first time. The greens were so much greener that December. When we first walked outside the air smelled like it did the day Brandon and I got locked up, a winter smell but without the signs of snow.

"What's your name, young?"

"Dwayne. You?" He told me Black. One moment I was an eleventh grader who'd never known a Black, the next I was in a car headed to prison: the land where brothers sport nicknames like new clothes. It was different from being at home, where the nickname always revealed something you already knew. When I asked the youngin beside me his name, and he said Black, that was his way of saying wasn't no other name important now. Just *Black*. Back then, I thought just being in that car meant I'd become the stereotype I thought I'd never be. Days when I looked at classmates who I thought had nothing going for them and nights I stood on corners with dudes selling drugs, always pulling back far enough so that I wasn't the one selling the stuff, led me to that car. I thought the labels they gave me in school, Talented and Gifted and such, made me exempt from the dull silver glint of the cuffs around my wrists, but I was in a car headed to prison before anyone I knew. I listened to Black, but my mind went in and out of my own troubles. He'd been to Southampton before for a short bid, the back end of an eighteen-month sentence. I wanted him to keep talking, to tell me what to look for, why he wanted to avoid the place and didn't think it was a big deal to be going there.

"How much time you got?"

The radio was on the *Russ Par Morning Show*. "Nine years." Russ Par was asking whether people in prison should be able to go to college. A woman called in and said that if she couldn't afford to go to college, there wasn't no way a man who robbed, shot up, killed somebody or stood on her corner selling crack should get to go. I thought about Black, on his second bid. Would he have been locked up if he'd gotten a college education in prison? College didn't keep Terrence Johnson from putting a bullet in his head. And it made me wonder if prison did something to you that a book couldn't repair. I remember the show now, how angry I was without knowing that the woman was eligible for the same money someone in prison got to go to college, and that the recidivism rate for people with college degrees is much lower than for those without. I couldn't argue with her in my head and think about going to prison. The deputies were talking about how it was bullshit to let these *stupid-ass young niggas running around with they pants down with no respect for they mamas do anything but more time.* Same time they were talking in the front Black was finishing up telling me how he had a five-year sentence as if it was short change. The whole world would change in five years though is what I thought, and maybe change twice while I did my nine years.

There was a club under the passenger seat. I saw its red hooked end near my feet. Before Black asked I let him know I was locked up for carjacking. The club reminded me of the car I stole, and how for one night I left it parked on my street with a club on it, as if it were mine, as if I would have been upset to see someone else pop its ignition and drive off like it was theirs. The care I took with that Grand Prix was ridiculous. Black told me I was crazy, a wild young nigga is what he said. But he must have known I was scared as I pushed the club around with my right foot and asked how Southampton was when he was there. I watched him look out the window. "Slim, you was lunching to do that shit."

And I must have been lunching. Black finally nodded off beside me. The deputy in the passenger seat slept, too. It was just the driver and me, and the driver wasn't much for words. He looked into the rearview mirror for approaching cars, not for my face.

Two years before my crime I read Nathan McCall's *Makes Me Wanna Holler*, the kind of book black women give their sons when teachers begin to call home too often, or when the police show up at the door to give a warning or when the word *truancy* becomes a word to be said at the dinner table. McCall, Malcolm X, Albert Sample and Claude Brown all famous because they had a story they could articulate about trouble and overcoming. Some folks just want to read the story, but many think there is something in there to save their sons, their nephews, their cousins. Maybe there is something. I'd read them all before a cop had the need to pull his pistol on me, read them before my mother had to take a day off of her job and go to my school to request letters of support from my teachers. I like to think that car ride was different for me, that because I carried all these images of prison in my head from books about black men who went in and came out I looked at things different. I wanted to know why all the books I read didn't keep me out of prison and didn't keep the cuffs from clamping over my wrists. But that didn't stop me from being shook, terrified and wanting to open my eyes to another reality. One hundred and twenty something pounds with ten books full of nightmares clanking around inside my head. I was running toward my past, toward every wrong turn no one could warn me away from.

My mom didn't give me McCall's book. She didn't think I needed the story of a young brother who came up hard. A woman gave me the book, somebody's mother who must have seen trouble in my eyes. In the way I talked, or walked. I don't know, just know I read it and was still in that car headed to the place McCall made famous.

When I opened McCall's book, it was to a savage beating he and his friends gave a white boy for being on their turf. The white boy rode his bike into Portsmouth, Virginia, because he didn't realize it wasn't safe. McCall and his boys let him know with their fists and the soles of their boots how unsafe it was. He called it "get-back."

Get-back for the soles of boots that had been thumping on the heads of black folks for years is what he said. McCall talked about a racism that dominated his life in a way different from mine. A visceral way. *Visceral*, it even sounds like a bike crashing on someone's head. I pulled the pistol on the sleeping white man because I thought I could do it and not have to live with it for the rest of my life. It wasn't get-back, although I'd picked a white man on purpose. His skin color made him a stranger to me, and I never considered that what I did to a stranger could color my life.

When I got to Fairfax I wanted to read the book again. In order to send it my mother first had to rip the hard cover off the book. The jail officials said that hardback books could be used as weapons. The first time I read the book I didn't realize that McCall only spent three years in prison. Even though that section about his imprisonment is less than a quarter of the book, it dominated my memories of the book. His story captured every reason why once you go to prison, it's with you forever, the invisible handshake you offer everyone you meet. Most of the men locked up around me on any given day were black. Blue-black, black-black, light-chocolate-colored black. Even the two deputies who drove me to prison were black. McCall's prison experience was the same, and I think the people who pass these books out to the young men they see in trouble expect that McCall explained this. He probably did explain it, too. I didn't notice though, because the book was entertainment for me; it wasn't about my life because I wasn't going to prison. When I came to the jail, I remembered his stories about robberies; I remembered his stories about what time did to him; I remembered when he pulled a razor blade on someone he had a beef with—he didn't bother talking, he just started swinging the blade around. I remembered Tooty, too, the young man from McCall's neighborhood who had a group of men run a train on him—meaning they lined up and raped him one at a time. I remembered all these details, even to the time McCall spent learning to use a printing press and how he felt making parole. I remembered those things the moment the cell door closed behind me, but never thought about them a second before I drove away in that white man's car. That's the burden of redemption. You write a book and hope in the small moments someone will remember what you say and put the gun down.

16

An Old Story

our mama don't wear no drawls," the voice called from beside the beat-up Crown Victoria. The laughter that followed came from there, too. "I saw her when she took them off." We were still laughing as we walked, and someone else yelled, "Standing in the welfare line eating swine . . ." It could have been any day of the week, but it was a Saturday and the sun drew sweat from my pores. "Trying look fine, with her stank behind." It was the spring of 1993, damn near summertime, those spring days when all I wanted was a cold gym and a bouncing basketball. I thought I was going to be Isiah Thomas, practiced pushing the orange ball I could never palm back and forth between my legs whenever I was moving. Raphael, Chris, Devon and I were walking away from the crate hanging from the steps behind the old Safeway. By then the peach fuzz we claimed was the start of beards and goatees meant we were too old to be shooting ball there, but every so often you could catch someone trying to pull the crate down with two hands.

That day it was us. When we left, we stepped through the fence, the same fence we'd stepped through for years walking away from that court.

We all headed toward Rochester Square. Sam was chilling in the front of the complex, talking to a couple people. You could say the past had revisited the neighborhood that day: the crate rattling with dunks and off-balance jumpers; Sam out in Lancaster, posted up on the corner where he used to be all the time; and me, out there like I still lived there. I hadn't been around there much since I started going to Walker Mill Middle School and moved. I hadn't seen Sam in a year.

"What's up y'all?"

"Ain't shit. I see you still think you know what to do with that basketball," Sam said, dumping ashes from his cigarette into the street. I heard Raphael tell him I moved and didn't come around much anymore. Everyone knew I played ball for William Beanes Elementary School's rec team again that year, but I hadn't been coming around to just sit on the fences and talk trash, or throw a football around in the streets. I wasn't with the boys I'd grown up with as everyone started rapping to girls and finding more ways to spend their time than with sports and video games. My life around there had become two hours of practice and then the walk home. It was the end of seventh grade and I'd just walked into the middle of a story. People looked at me as if I was interrupting something, and the attention turned from me back to Sam soon as the "where you beens" were over. Sam, dark skin with a head that had been bald and gleaming for as long as I'd known him, was the first black dude I knew to put black nail polish on his fingernails and still be cool. He did it just to do it and had others following him. He didn't look like it standing in this parking lot, flicking ashes from a Newport into the wind, but Sam was good at everything we thought important. Everybody knew that on the court his handle was nice, he played football, and probably could play baseball, too, if anyone around here ever had a bat, glove or ball. Plus, he could throw his hands. His skills made him a legend.

When he started to speak, I wondered if anyone there knew how old he was. I didn't. Sam said, "The police, them muthafuckas just be fucking with niggas for no reason." Everyone nodded their head in agreement. Even though the police had never harassed me, I knew people who'd been fucked up by them, dudes my age and my size beaten over the head for running, running because they didn't trust the police. "Last weekend we were out chilling. Taking our time, you know. It wasn't nothing serious either, just rolling around thinking 'bout what we were gonna do. I had my folks' car, so niggas wasn't dirty and wasn't nobody thinking about the police 'cause we was chilling. Sirens came out of nowhere."

"Shit, sirens don't never come out of nowhere. They some shit you expect even when you ain't expecting it," Devon, skinnier than the pole beside us that holds up the light, was still talking shit. He was right. No one there remembered being surprised by sirens. Just something you hear, and when you hear it you realize you expected to hear it and need to decide to either run or walk in the other direction. The thing is, Sam was saying he didn't expect to be fucked with, and that's what's important to this story.

"When the police pull us over, I'm cool. Shit, we weren't dirty and I'm thinking stay calm. You know over there off of Marlboro Pike, by the carryout? We were pulling out of the carryout. I had fries with mumbo sauce in my lap. You'd think everyone coming in and out of the carryout had coke stashed in the cut. That's what the cop said, a white cop, when they pulled us over, "Where's your stash?" His partner was white, too. He asked for my license, but then he was like fuck it, all of you get outta the car. By then I was mad as shit. He ain't even looked good at my license or registration and had me getting outta the car. What? Maybe I did look at the muthafucka wrong. But look, when they slammed the three of us on the ground, I felt like the shit was my fault. Five, six minutes we on the curb in cuffs."

Nobody was talking but Sam. I'd heard stories about the PG police before, but was thinking "damn, for real" when Sam said the police had smacked him upside the head with his nightstick. Hearing a story from the person it happened to changes your reaction to it, makes you less removed. Sam said they did the shit for fun, not even to beat up on him bad, just to be like, "yeah, and what the fuck you gonna do about it." The Rodney King verdict was a year old but the police around the way had long been notorious for gifting bruises and weren't going to stop because of a riot on the other side of the country.

"So what you do?" People stared at me when I asked, but I'm thinking that he had to do something. I wasn't thinking that he'd say when they got back in the car tears ran down his face, that anger left him gripping the steering wheel so tight that the ridges left marks on his palms.

"I was heated and didn't start the car for a second, just sat there with my head on the wheel. My shit was hurting for real. He left a little bruise over my eye, but nothing that couldn't be explained away. Anyway, who was I gonna tell? The police got my name on they files for some shit or another I know, so who was gonna believe me? I was like fuck it, let's get us a vic." Sam smoked his Newport and looked out at the street. He was always looking out at the street, waiting for someone or expecting something. I didn't know what he was talking about. Where was he going to get a vic, and how was that going to get back at the police? When he started talking again, Sam told us that they drove out to Montgomery County, 'cause it was nothing but white folks out there. I was young. This was the first time that I'd heard about a robbery, first time I realized that people I knew robbed others. All Sam's anger toward the police was taken out on an unsuspecting white couple in a county I'd never been to. He described it to us. How they pulled up to the red light kinda slow, making sure they were the first car at the light. He told us he wasn't driving then, that he let somebody else drive so he could get outta the car. I listened with a mix of fascination and surprise. Because this wasn't a movie, this was a story being told in Rochester Square.

"It was a white couple in a Max or an Accord. The car didn't even matter. When I flashed the burner the dude's eyes damn near went to the back of his head. Wasn't nobody else on the street. Shawn pulled the pump out." Shawn went to school with me, an eighth grader. I thought to myself, "What the fuck is he doing running around with a shotgun." This was before *Menace II Society* and the flashing lights that made some people think carjacking was cool. This was the suburbs of Maryland. I was stunned to hear how anger pushed somebody I admired to pull a pistol on a white man. And the thing was, the victim's race was the whole point of the story. White cop, white victim. It didn't matter if the gun, the fear, the robbery didn't resolve the oppression that was felt as much as that we were passing on to each other a warped way of dealing with anger that we didn't know we had.

Rochester Square had changed from the place it was during my early childhood games. Rather than just hearing rumors about violence trickle down fifth-hand from someone's cousin's uncle's brother, I was now listening to the one with the gun in his hand tell the story. Some of the boys I grew up with were now the boys my mom always told me to avoid. But I couldn't avoid them because we'd had the birthday parties together, the pizza parties, and they weren't just thugs who could be dismissed. It was Sam telling the story. Sam, who made sure that even though I was the smallest dude in the neighborhood I played football with everyone else, 'cause I could catch, even if I was scared to get hit. Now here I was twelve years old and I was starting to see the complicated space that I lived in, where people you thought you knew could be out there doing things you'd never imagine. That day, as Sam talked, he told us about the look on the man's face when he put his pistol so close to his lips that he could kiss it. Then told us how afterward they blew the car up in a field in Capital Heights. I still think about how they made the street that white man probably lived on the most dangerous place he'd ever been. I can see him on the curb, just like the police had Sam and them, shaking and crying, the boy just a year older than me holding a shotgun over him.

Sam told me his story. That's it. He didn't put a gun in my hand, and the story didn't have me hanging out on street corners until the moon faded from sight, but it did open up the small realm of possibility for what I thought a teenager could do. It made Shawn wild, too young to be running so wild, but wild. That was the first time I'd gotten the crime story firsthand. And it was the first time the crime had a tint of something beyond craziness to it.

Years later, after I ran up on the man asleep in his car, I wanted to use Sam's story to explain why I chose to rob a white man in the middle of an empty parking lot. Why I searched out a white man, but it wouldn't work. The police hadn't abused me, and my anger wasn't nearly as fierce as his. And that's part of the reason why even though Sam's story was in my head every time I wanted to explain my crime to my mother, I left it there. Because, in the end, I know that my tapping on that innocent man's window was a twisted way for me to tap on my own head, a way to wake myself up from the dream I'd lived for a night. A dream where I'd convinced myself that to be wild with a pistol was something other than to be criminal. Maybe I only really started to wake up when I was headed toward Southampton with the judge's voice still fresh in my ears, telling me that I could get something out of my years of cuffs if I chose.

17

Prison 101: SRC, an Intro

Everyone who leaves a jail in the state of Virginia is sent to a receiving center before being shipped to a prison. This was where they issue ID cards and state numbers, where you have that special shower where you are doused with white powder that kills lice. The receiving center isn't a permanent place, just a transition spot as the system gathers information on you to determine at what prison you'd be spending your time. Southampton Receiving Center was the receiving center most of the young men went to; anyone who was under twenty-five usually found themselves there. That first day when Black and I arrived they brought us into a room with a handful of other inmates. Lieutenant Brown, shorter by a head than most of us, yelled and spat the routine as he saw it while we waited to know what would happen next. I didn't know it then, but the scar that ran along Brown's neck was placed there when he screamed at the wrong person. They said a young boy tried to chop his head off. That's how they told me the story, "This cat from Richmond was trying to chop his muthafuckin head off. Almost did, too." Brown wanted us to be scared as he ordered us to strip naked in groups of twos and step under a shower to get sprayed with the delousing agent. It was the first time I'd been naked around another man. Prison life is a series of small indignities that you're made to adapt to. I really didn't want to do this, but I did anyway. In the jail we all talked about how we'd be the bad nigga who made up his own rules to follow, but from day one I learned there really weren't any bad niggas. The most any of us could hope for was a Bigger Thomas moment when we bucked the system and pulled out a blade to shut up whoever ran their mouth or waved their fists for a second too long.

After the shower, we were issued a blue jumpsuit and a pair of brown leather work boots that were made at Augusta Correctional Center. In a small room with women working behind computers, we were issued identification cards with the numbers that would follow us for the rest of our bid. 251534—that was my number. The woman who issued my card didn't say it was more important than my name. She just told me I'd need to have that card to get visits, and I'd need to have that number on any mail or money order I received to get it. She told me that a letter received with just the number would get to me just the same. We sat before these women and took our neat little ID cards and slipped them in our pockets, happy not to be cuffed. Not smiling, but not seething either. That's what it means to *bid*. You get lost in the motions of things you have to do to survive and forget you're just surviving, even when all you're doing is going through standard procedures to be placed in another cell. Subconsciously, without any real thought, I learned that number before I was put in a cell: 251534. I even noticed that the person before me had the number 251532, and wondered if that meant there were a hundred thousand people locked up.

They housed us in one of three units, or wings. They put me in a cell on A wing, with Tony, the Puerto Rican dude who had the number 251532. Tony could name every street in Richmond and spoke English and Spanish as first languages. I didn't think there were Puerto Ricans in Richmond. Prison, already, was becoming the most diverse place I'd ever been to. Standing in the hallway, I could reach my arms out and put a hand on the cell on each side of me. Christmas was around the corner, my second one locked up. And I was getting the strangest of gifts, we all were: a world that was smaller than our dreams and memories, memories that didn't mean anything to our families and meant too much to us.

We were deep, the black boys at the receiving center making up more than ninety percent of the folks there. Each wing may have had a couple of white boys, maybe a Latino, but more than anything else we were black. Within a week they'd tested our blood and given us an IQ test. They didn't tell anyone what the tests were for, and because the IQ test cut into the short amount of time we had to go outside, most people marked anything in a hurry to leave the room. They probably created statistics about our intelligence with those tests. We were restless, a roomful of young men who'd been in jails all over Virginia, where we'd been unable to get outside for more than a second and didn't care about the results of an IQ test. Part of me wanted to know my IQ; I wanted the test to say I was some kind of genius.

We had names: Charles, Rashid, Wise, Victory, BJ, Tony, Marcel, Muhammad, Dawud, Yusef, Divine, Roger, Lil Man, Big Pete, Treetop, Ant. And more names, names that I can't remember, but stories I do. The boy whose brother was with me at Landmark Detention Center who could braid his own hair. The tall brother who had a jump shot from anywhere on the court, and the light-skinned dude from New York who had a first step that made me rethink my skills. I remember pieces of their lives as we found out what it meant to be inmates together. I remember the morning they called us all into a makeshift movie room. Just a small room that doubled as the church, with rows of chairs. We were there that day for a talk about prison. A woman, younger and prettier than any woman should be allowed to be when talking to a group of young prisoners, was talking about diseases.

"It is imperative that you get tested and you get tested regularly. There is an increased chance that one will develop hepatitis A, B and C while in prison."

Beside me, Marcel was talking shit. I'd met him a few days before. He was from Norfolk somewhere but didn't know any of the other dudes from Norfolk on our wing and wasn't territorial with it. He kept calling out, "Who is 'one' and what the fuck is hepatitis, and why they got three levels of that shit." I didn't know what hepatitis was either, and I wanted to know why it was so prevalent in prison.

The woman talking attracted more attention than what she was saying. All around me dudes were whispering about her breasts or her ass. She said that the rate of HIV was six times higher in prison than on the street. A month before I came in I found out one of the dudes I'd been smoking weed with for a year had HIV. He didn't say HIV though. It was one night when blunts had been passed around and around, and some old heads, who weren't really old, just in their twenties, were in the cut smoking boat. I don't know what led to him saying it. But he bugged out and then started talking about some-body fucking his girl. Said she had that shit. That's how he said it, she had that shit. Said he had it, too. Now here was this woman tell-ing me that the rate of infection was six times higher in prison. *Rate of infection*, another phrase that exists within the frame of prison in my head, forever associated with this beautiful woman, who stood before us knowing many of us wouldn't touch a woman for years, telling us about the risk, the threat of HIV.

She didn't have to say how some of us would get it. I walked out of the small movie room thinking about women, HIV and homosexuality.

After we left, no one said much. We all knew that you got HIV from having sex with men in prison. Simple as that. If you decided early on not to do it, you cut your risk down by a hundred percent. As long as the decision stayed in your hands. Hepatitis was a different beast. I got locked up and learned things I didn't know existed could kill me. No one in that room was over twenty, twenty-one. No one wanted to hear about three or four more things that could kill you besides the time already hanging over your head. That's why people just kept it moving. And if fear did have a clutch on someone's head, they hid it. I thought about the judge, and how he told me he was under no illusion prison would help me, but I could get something out of it if I wanted to. He wasn't talking about HIV but I could get that, and so far that's all the prison officials and guest speakers had informed me that prison had to offer: a shot at a few diseases that could lock my name into a different category of statistic.

I struggled to get by. I was locked up in a new world. It turned out Brandon was in a different wing and at first we rarely saw each other. Some days stretched to night with us only leaving the cell for breakfast, lunch and dinner. Suddenly, I wasn't locked out of a cell all day, but locked inside a cell. There was only one dayroom that the three units shared and from the inside of the cell it seemed like we never got out.

We probably went outside every other day, or every third day. Outside. The rec yard. At the beginning, life there was split into two worlds: outside and inside. Outside was the rec yard. It was the dayroom. It was the three trips we made each day to the dining hall. It was even the minutes we spent out of the cell as we walked to the showers. That set of four showerheads and no curtains. If you wanted to get clean, you stripped down to nothing. Bare-assed in front of the other three in the shower, the two or three or four drying themselves just outside the range of water and the four getting ready to step in once you stepped out. All of that made up the outside world. When you got to look in someone's eyes.

The other world, the inside world, was anything that you heard or saw while in a jail cell. It's where I first learned that you could make a radio antenna from a soda can ripped into long strips and hung, with a scrap of tape salvaged from a letter, to the ceiling. Marcel showed me how to make an antenna and how to drape it from the ceiling in hopes of catching an hour or two of a station in Norfolk. The inside was back on the wing where trash talk about who had game and who didn't made up most of the conversation. That and the threats of who was going to get their shit split open for a wrong look. That and war stories traded back and forth by people who knew each other by more than the nicknames that sounded off at odd times during the day. Absolut. Righteous. Wishbone. Steel. Peanut. Fats. Unique. Twin. Smith. Jones. Foots. A running string of names that formed the place where the cultures we left on the streets met and combined with the cultures I was beginning to learn. Nicknames and attributes. Attributes, nothing but a way to pull a Malcolm X and reject the name your mother gave you. Everyone was calling birth names government names, like we were all named by the federal government and not by women still wet with blood. At first I didn't understand any of this. Just knew that I had a bag of food in my room, a top bunk with crisp white sheets and a rack of noise to help me remember where I'd be on Christmas.

18

The Mathematics of
Reunions and a Nation

Brandon worked in the kitchen. He slipped onto the wing once or twice to holler at me, but we couldn't talk unless I was on the rec yard. On the yard, the two full courts gave us all the opportunity to sweat out our frustration in a way that we remembered. The first time we talked, Brandon walked on the rec yard wearing kitchen whites and carrying a photo album. The album was filled with our peers and looking at them I couldn't help but think of the class trips, the homecomings, the prom and all the other things I'd miss while in prison. Around me there were young boys with thirty and forty years and I had to put the time the judge had given us in perspective. Being twenty-five when I came home wouldn't be as bad as being fifty. When I looked up I noticed that from where we stood the barbed wire coiled around the fences looked close enough to touch.

"Anyone from around the way up here?" I asked.

"Nah, it's not too many people from 'round the way down here. You know Peanut? Yeah, I know Alexandria ain't 'round the way, but northern Virginia, D.C., Maryland, all that shit the same down here." While he talked, I flipped through the photo album. He had pictures of a few girls we went to school with, a few others he'd met through people up there and random shit I hadn't seen in like a year. For the most part his pictures were a part of a world we'd left, a world that I'd shut myself away from.

"I haven't written a letter to anyone from school since a month into this bid. I just pulled back. Recognized the shit that was going on in here wasn't conversation pieces, and I didn't want to hear about what was happening out there. Someone writes me telling me about our class trip and what I'm 'posed to say back? I was in the hole reading a letter and the shit had me so frustrated I tried to punch a hole in the wall."

He looked at me. It was a "you lunching" look, but it was also one of those "yeah, I know how shit be" looks. I told him after I tried to slip my fist between the cracks in the wall that I just stopped writing letters. My peers and I were suddenly in different worlds, with time going at the same rate but working a different kind of magic on me than it was on them. For a minute talking with Brandon gave me the rhythms of the world I'd lost, and I understood how the people on the wing locked up with friends had it a little easier. They could pass back and forth the names of streets and shared landmarks and go to sleep with a little bit of home each night. Sometimes the rest of the wing would quiet down, and I knew people weren't sleeping. People weren't listening to the radio; the COs snatched up the makeshift antennas so often that most people didn't bother with them, and even if you had one you could only get the radio if you stood with one foot in the air and your arm stretched to the window. It was like a rerun of the bunny rabbit antenna days with the black-and-white TVs. I know people were sitting back in their cell, unable to stop themselves from just listening. I listened. That's why I recognized what it felt like to hear home in somebody's slang, and why I appreciated being able to say, "You remember Shanda?" and get a laugh in response. That moment made every time we saw each other a reunion of sorts.

Listening to the voices on the hall gave me a constant sense of what was lost. The body. The ability to give someone dap, to shake a hand just as you hear their voice yelling, "What's up." That was gone. None of us could walk to the 7-Eleven 'cause we wanted to. Being in a prison in the South removed me from not only my school, family and friends, but also my memories of them. The conversations about the streets I walked, the bus stops I sat at and everything else that went along with being a kid in PG County were gone. This was the price I paid every day. It was the reverberation of the night a pistol fit into the curve of my palm like a woman's breast. The letters were still coming from home, from my family, but at the time my mind was more concerned with adjusting. Someone else would call it getting institutionalized, getting used to having a cell door close behind me every day. It wasn't getting institutionalized though, it was learning a way to deal with living on a wing with thirty strangers, all young, and all wrestling with personal issues and the time the judge had handed out. At night, when the mail came around, I freed my mind and went to wherever the letters took me, but during the day, it was prison. And prison was sweating the laundryman for a jumpsuit a size bigger, and a pair of boots that were fresh, so fresh I could leave the strings unlaced and pretend I had on a pair of Timberlands.

We didn't move around much. It was a world in four places: the showers, the cafeteria, the movie room or the rec yard. I kept my eyes open, surprised that no knives were flying. No fists either. Not really. The one thing I always noticed were the young brothers who talked about doing the *math*—Victory, Wise, Star and a kid we called Night. After count they'd be on the door talking in a string of words shouted out in a pattern that sounded incomprehensible. *God Cipher Now Absolut Divine Equality.* Half the time I only heard a word or two. They made language dance to a beat only they could keep up with, and held long conversations in a spoken Morse code. Ever since I was a kid I'd been into mysteries. Sherlock Holmes, Dashiell Hammett, Walter Mosley. Any detective writer I could get my hands on I'd read. I watched *Matlock, Perry Mason*. It wasn't always for the action, but for the figuring out what the deal was. The whodunit. And whenever I got interested in school, it was because I got the feeling of wanting to know how and why. That's what listening to those dudes did for me. Most of them were my age but they knew something I didn't, and they believed what they knew would save them.

It wasn't exactly religion. And it wasn't a gang either, although sometimes, posted up in groups of four and six and eight with a severity and discipline that didn't mesh with the oversized jumpsuits and state numbers they sported, you could mistake them for a gang. Except they were always talking about *doing the knowledge*. And while I had no idea what that meant, I knew it meant that what was important to them wasn't the violence that had put most of us in prison.

There's something about waking up every morning to your life in a box that makes you want to learn to be more than you were when you went to sleep the night before. The judges all up and down the Tidewater and Richmond areas had been handing out football numbers for crimes that just a few years before were guaranteed to get you no more than five, ten years. Maybe twenty, but twenty meant you had a shot at parole after seven. But then, once parole had been abolished in the late nineties, a twenty-year sentence turned into life. And it seemed like more than half the people around me had over twenty years. A twenty-year-old, eighteen-year-old, seventeen-year-old on his way to prison, just arriving: it's almost natural he's going to want to find God and get real close to him to make that time easier. And even if that's not the reason, if it's some con man's hustle to keep the fear of getting robbed or raped at bay, that's cool, too. Even then, I felt those fears nagging at my consciousness, so there's no way I can blame someone for gaining religion for safety. The problem was how prison had all of us shaping our identities around survival and the psychosis of a cell door closing. All I wanted was a way to deal with waking up and not understanding how the world, the landscape and everything I recognized was different.

THE TRUTH ABOUT A CELL

One morning I woke and realized the sun wasn't shooting light into the cell. In my head the body on the bed beneath me wasn't there. There was nothing but my breathing disrupting the air. There was no snoring, instead the off-and-on noise of three bluebirds calling. Bluebirds or mockingbirds. And I thought if I opened my eyes I would walk out of the door and jump in the shower. Get ready for school. It's senior year.

But none of it was to be. The cell played tricks with my mind that vanished when the lights on the wing came on signaling count would occur soon. My cell partner snored beneath me. I'd never seen a bluebird or a mockingbird. I felt the mosquitoes, the lumps they'd left on my skin. I knew that in ten minutes someone would walk past the cell with a flashlight. They always came early. The snoring body below made me remember that I'd never had a brother. No one I had to share a toilet and a bathroom with. But sharing a cell with a man wasn't having a brother. The stories we passed back and forth were always about something out of reach. An early release date. The hand of some girl we used to talk to back in the day.

Tony told me he would have never gotten locked up if his family had stayed in Puerto Rico. He said Puerto Rico was home. I didn't have a place to say that would have saved me. I didn't think there was anything for me to be saved from. Maybe that cell, that conversation and dreams that leave bluebirds and mockingbirds made me hunger for a life I never knew. I closed my eyes as if I was dreaming, as if there was something that I could do in sleep to make what I was waking up to change. They wanted us to stand up for count, and if we wouldn't stand they'd give us a charge, a yellow slip of paper that said we broke a rule. And for breaking the rule we'd lose a privilege as if there was something more that we could lose once we'd given away our freedom.

In sleep I could pretend. Instead of hearing the bell that signaled two guards standing at the end of the wing ready to begin count, I heard bluebirds raising their pitch. Instead of the flashlights that beat on the door, I heard mockingbirds. Instead of a cellmate under me, it was me alone sleeping on the top bunk. The bunk bed my mother's way of telling me something she could never tell me. The bunk bed the secret to imagining a loss that I could never get. Until now.

There was nothing that could balance out the sense of loss. But some things kept my mind off of it. Wise had walked into the reception center with a bag of Donald Goines books he'd gotten at the jail. Everyone on the wing read them, even guys who hadn't read in years. I ran through them, forgetting much of what they were about as I read but noticing how so much of what he was writing, even when it was about violence and death, was about race and about the options he thought black men had. The books always ended in death, as if death was a cure to the violence. But it wasn't, and years after he'd written his books most of us were in cells having relived one of his tales, if only for a moment.

When the Goines books were gone, I started reading whatever was in the library. It wasn't a real library, just a room with books haphazardly thrown all over the place. In a real way my mind was starving and I was reading anything I could put my hands on to keep it from atrophying. I didn't know then but this would become the story of my life in prison. In a lot of ways when I started running with the group of boys that called themselves Five Percenters it was to keep my mind from breaking down from inactivity. I was attracted to the confidence these young brothers exuded, to their language and ways. They called themselves gods in a world of cuffs and closing cell doors—and they made *doing the knowledge* seem the blueprint for survival. I never prayed or looked around corners for miracles, except once. And since I'd ended up at the receiving center just like everyone else, I'd pretty much given up on the idea of God as a balled-up fist ready to swing at the faces of folks scowling at me. I kept looking back and realizing again and again that the gun in my palm that night was the reason I was in prison. I'd carjacked a white man while he slept in his car. I had a pistol. I pled guilty. My family thought it would pan out different, my lawyer did, too, and probably, on some level, I expected to go home. But charges read to a judge the way they read.

The point is that I had to find a way to deal with the world I was in and the world I'd left every night. I looked around me and the Five Percenters seemed to be dealing with time better than others. They'd fashioned a language to describe the world that was different from what I'd known, and it was partially the language that these six or seven brothers used in private conversations and out in the open that I wanted to learn. They told me they were building, and I thought it meant they were finding a way to survive.

Prison made language the most important thing in the world. Back then, I called everyone youngin. *Youngin*, the word I'd inherited from Swann Road and Suitland and D.C. and all the young brothers I hung around. When I got to Southampton and started recognizing differences in folks, the way they spoke and talked, *youngin* didn't always work. At first it was just choice. I watched two dudes arguing over a name:

Who the fuck you calling stickman?

You nigga.

Me, nah, you ain't talking to me. Say that shit when the doors pop.

If you didn't have the key to decipher the language it all sounded like noise. In the mornings we walked to breakfast and it was the slang that separated us into groups. The three people who peppered their conversation with *stickman* were all from Richmond, the two of us who said *youngin* were from D.C. And anyone that said *blood* had been talking to men older than himself. If someone called you brother, they just didn't want to call you nigga. *Brother* didn't mean anything, just a play on words that could be spoken by the dude ready to split your head open or watch someone else do it.

It was in the cafeteria that the Five Percenters stood out. They used words like *sun, god* and *star.* They said *god-body* and *standing on the square.* And there, at the reception center, with just two hundred of us total, they moved with a crispness, a knife-blade military precision. It made me think about the power invested in what you call someone. To understand it you have to picture a prison cafeteria. A serving line with seven inmates ready to slop heaps of red, green or brownish mush on your plate. The noise has been ratcheted up to a level where conversations are yelled, not spoken. In the middle of this, six young men walk in with their hands in some kind of configuration before them or behind their backs. Even though everyone else would be screaming, or almost screaming, they'd be calm. Hardly talking, and though they are wearing the blue jumpsuit we all wear, for some reason theirs look different. The one in the front, with little tiny twists that are threatening to be dreads, calls out, "Thank you, brother," as he gets his food. None of them look at the guards, except to examine them, pointing out little things to themselves like who has on the Masonic ring. Then they sit, untroubled by the chaos that builds as the room fills. They call each other *god* and *sun* and filled the air with the sacrilegious. They believed they were god and if there was a truth to that I wanted to know it. Whatever they were, they were making their lives into something different from the Donald Goines tales that swirled around the wings. I saw them moving through trouble like with a secret that I needed.

They were gravity to me. I was always on the outskirts of their conversation. Or asking someone something about it. Pushing at their rules to see how much I could find out without saying, "Okay, I want to be down." Because even though I wanted to know, I thought being down with anything was looked at as weakness. I wanted to stand on my own two, and I wanted to know about the thing before I started committing myself to it. There remained a lot that I couldn't know though. That idea, the thought that *building* meant carrying yourself to a place that was better than where you were. *Building*. It pulled at me. The language they owned, the lexicon that made *math* and *science* something that got skimmed off of the muck and shit that happened every day, and that could be learned without a graphing calculator, was a mystery that fucked with my head for days on end.

19

Names and Naming

One day I walked out of the cell and heard three people talking about a meeting that would be going on that night. One of them was saying that if you wanted to hear the truth you should come. Christmas was all in the air: it was the rusty bitterness at being locked up that I tasted in the mornings before I brushed my teeth, and the tension that knotted the muscles in my shoulders as my cell partner and I did our push-ups in the cell. Every night we did two hundred. Then we'd lie on the floor under the bunk and bench press the bunk. He'd pull one end up as I got in position under it and gripped the metal bar with my hands. Once I had it, he let it go and I pushed hard. It probably didn't weigh all that much and we were only lifting one end but it felt like work and that's what we needed. That innovation was happening in some kind of way in every cell to beat back the blues. Or it was happening in the church services, or the religious meeting like the one I'd just heard about.

I went to the meeting to get out of the cell for a few minutes or an hour. I was curious, looking for a way to get somewhere without knowing where I wanted to go. In the meeting ten or so young brothers sat in a circle. The one who everyone seemed to be looking toward for direction wore a white hat, a kufi. I remembered tenth grade. The summer. I'd gone to Kings Dominion, the huge amusement park in Virginia, with a friend and was rocking a kufi. At the time, it was a D.C. thing. I'd seen someone wearing one and adopted the style. Never mind that I didn't know any person who was Muslim. At Kings Dominion a brother walked up to me and said, "A-Salaam-Alaikum." The sun was a razor cutting wide stripes of light out of the shadows around me, the funnel cake in my hand was dripping with strawberry syrup. "Yeah, what's up, man." He didn't scream on me or nothing. Just stepped off. I didn't halfway make out his greeting and only knew what it meant because I'd seen *Malcolm X*. I wondered what that brother thought that day two years ago as I watched Rashid. He was the one at the head of the circle wearing the white kufi, with a book in his hand.

"This is the Quran. Written down and printed exactly as it was told to Muhammad hundreds of years ago." He went on like that for a minute. The history of this book that was like the Bible. He said that the people who followed the Quran were Muslims. As we read the Quran I could see some people could barely read, some could read but couldn't process the ideas behind the stories and some were on point. There were ten, maybe twelve of us in a small room, and for an hour or so we weren't in prison. Being hard wasn't as important as knowing the meaning of a word, or the importance of a passage. Even though I hadn't expected to walk into a class about Islam, I stayed because it felt good to be free of the fears and obsessions that had begun to drive my thinking.

The class was a part of Ramadan, the Islamic holy month when all adults and capable children fast from sunup to sundown each day and increase the time spent studying and reading the Quran.

One night Rashid told us, "A thousand years ago, the Quran was revealed to Muhammad." He said Muhammad couldn't read, and that the Quran was a revelation from Allah. Part of me wanted to believe that Allah would whisper a book into my ear, into anyone's ear, but it was hard. I didn't believe in much of anything and was just searching. Not for an identity. Not to find myself. But for a place inside the walls where it was acceptable to be myself. I was seventeen years old and liked reading books. My life had shifted from thoughts of college to which prison was the sweetest, to which prison I could go to and have the easiest bid. What I knew was that in that dusty room, which was a storage closet any other day, I didn't have to be in prison. I could close my eyes and listen to Rashid sound the call to prayer, or listen to him start reading from the Quran, and when I opened my eyes I looked around at the brothers intently reading or asking questions with no shame of being ridiculed for what they didn't know, without fear of being laughed at for stuttering while they read. Here I decided to try fasting. I listened to Rashid tell me how Ramadan was more than thirty days of fasting.

As regularly as I went to those classes it was never about faith. It wasn't about fronting either. You walk into a room with everyone seeming to believe with their whole being in something and you want that faith. It was true, I liked to read and to learn and this was the only community that I found doing this—but I also thought there was a chance that something would move me. I wanted to learn about the thing I'd walked into. I didn't decide to become a Muslim, but I decided to learn everything I could about it. I spent a day learning the tenets of Islam and reading the packet that he gave us about the history. I read more about Muhammad, but there weren't any good books in our library that went into his life. I read more of the Quran and saw how the stories were mirrors of the stories in the Bible. Someone may have been able to find the differences, the subtleties that made them different, but I couldn't. I learned the prayers, the height of the sun during each prayer and exactly how to prostrate my body as I repeated the words of each prayer. Reciting the prayer was like saying a poem.

The Muslims believed Allah was God and followed the teachings outlined by the Quran. They gave themselves new names that they wore like badges. The names signified all of Allah's attributes, his divine qualities. Our old names were government names, slave names, the white man's names. We never called the old names the names our mamas and daddies sweated over. The names of our aunts and uncles passed down to us. The vision that we were gaining, adopting, didn't leave room for nuance. You accepted the doctrine or you rejected it. When Rashid gave me the small book, *The 99 Attributes of Allah*, I got excited. To choose my own name, I thought maybe it could erase some of the past. As the stories of beat-downs given and guns drawn flowed in and out of the spiritual conversations, I realized that whatever I was, I wasn't the b-boy tough guy who would give someone a bloody nose. I thought it was cool to be able to pick a name that would represent who I was and wanted to be. I didn't know what Reginald meant, didn't know what Dwayne meant. I would learn, but not then, not in that cafeteria. So I perused the book, thought about names, how they fell from my mouth and hit the air. I thought about Faulkner's Bryon, and how he said a name was more than the sound for who a man was, but that it somehow augured what a man would do if other men could read the meaning in time.

The fiftieth attribute of Allah was Ash-Shahid. Shahid. The witness, the one who nothing is absent from. Ash. I didn't know what it meant, but I read it and thought fire. I thought James Baldwin. Shahid. I tested it out in the air. At Fairfax I'd decided to be a writer. An ink pen was the only way to carve a voice out of the air and have others hear it while in prison. Writers were witnesses. I wanted people to call me Shahid. I didn't add anything else onto it. I wasn't about to be Shahid Ahmad or Shahid Muhammad. I felt like if I added a last name I would be saying too much. Rejecting too much of myself. I wasn't ready to do that, but I was ready to become someone I wasn't when I walked into the jail. I wasn't sure how Shahid would work, but I christened myself. It wasn't that I became another person, but rather that I knew I wouldn't survive moving and thinking as I had before.

The day I decided on my name, I walked out of the cell and gave Rashid his book back.

All it took to become a Muslim was to say the Shahaddah. They were magic words in a way. The words were a proclamation that the speaker believed that there was only one God and Muhammad was his last prophet. It scared me that it was that easy to become something, just like it had always scared me that all I had to do to become Christian was repeat a similar chant and replace Muhammad's name with Jesus. I did it, but in a minute I was pulling back. Not from the fasting but from the commitment. I thought if you could become somebody else just by chanting words, you weren't really becoming someone else. I kept at it, thinking that something in me would move, but it didn't.

It was a hard month, that December. The fasting, the meetings and the constant feeling that I wasn't finding my place. I hadn't grown up religious, like many of the people around me, and that was a double-edged sword. What it meant was that I didn't have a problem opening my mind to what the Muslim brothers or Five Percenters said, but it also meant that I was finding myself in a place where people lose themselves more often than not. I'd had my ears half open to Christianity my whole life so I knew what they were talking about. We were nothing but two hundred kids running around dealing with issues of life and death literally and metaphorically and being seventeen with no spiritual foundation I wanted to cling to something that meant I was free. I knew Brandon grew up in the church and that what Rashid was kicking made no sense to him, and that what the folks were saying who called themselves god meant less. I could understand that, too, but it was good for me that Brandon didn't look at any of us as fools. It was all about sanity and survival. I listened to Rashid talking about the afterlife and realized that there was a real possibility the next time half the room listening would be free was in an afterlife. There wasn't a scripture in any book that was going to make me understand Randy having fifty-two years for a body, or Slim having fifteen for robbing a drug dealer. I wasn't going to speak on it out loud, 'cause that meant I had to argue over the sincerity of what they felt, but I wasn't ready to feel so strongly about anything that would happen after I returned to the dirt. I was too bitter about what was happening to me while I was alive.

I'd look around me. At Rashid. At Brandon. At all these young dudes who came into prison with a spiritual foundation. Folks who knew where to dive when they picked up a Bible or Quran before anyone told them. I admired them for that. But then I couldn't help but wonder what it was that caused a young dude to do something that's so against everything his family believed in, everything he believed in. Why did I do something that was against everything I believed in? The court system, the judge, he was probably thinking about how I didn't offer an answer to that kind of question when he sent me to prison. That's why so many of us were burying our heads in the books and religions that kept our families safe. I couldn't do it.

I was still looking for something else. It was too early for me to see the politics of it all. I still had the Five Percenters, who were telling me they had a truth that wasn't in the Bible or Quran. I was thinking that truth would have kept me out of prison and would keep me safe in it, if only I could figure it out.

20

Finally, the Knowledge or Something Close to It

hristmas dinner. The plates had a whole chicken on them is what I thought. The meat was falling off the bone and my fingers were in my mouth before I sat down. Everybody was missing home, but this meal was doing something. It put us in a place between depression and satiety. How do you tell someone you want more of something in a prison? That the meal was so good that it made you think you could push your chair away, get up and walk outside to the corner store. We couldn't walk away from that meal though; no matter how good it was, the taste of the chicken was just a reminder that our joy was rationed now. Handed out to us in little pieces that we had to claim with caution. I didn't know chickens came that big. It filled up over half the plate. Someone told me it was a capon.

A capon is a rooster castrated so that its meat becomes more ten-der and its behavior tame. We were in the kitchen hall, at least ten of us under eighteen, all of us under twenty-one. It was Christmas and we were salivating over a rooster who had its balls snatched at six weeks, trying not to think of the ways the judge's sentence castrated us. Early in all our bids and already we'd lived things we would not recover from. Even then I was afraid one day I'd want outta the cell and go crazy, beating on it until my knuckles bled. I thought I'd catch a mean case of claustrophobia. We were all in line waiting to see if the system would castrate us, eating capons and not knowing what they were. Just knowing they were good, that we wanted seconds.

needed a job. My mother didn't have money to send me every week, and even if she did I understood that I needed to make my own. I put in an application and the next thing I knew I had a job working in the kitchen. It meant getting up early, or getting up earlier, and serving food and sweeping floors and making twenty cents an hour and being talked to as if I was nothing by the kitchen supervisor, but I had a job.

Nothing in the world I was in made any sense, but making my own money, even if it was change on the dollar, meant I bought the chips and cakes in my footlocker. The price of my lawyer was still a hand in my mom's pocket. She gave the man thousands of dollars expecting me to come home, and all I'd seen since he cashed those checks were more jail cells, more prison cells. The sad thing was my sentence didn't even mean that my lawyer wasn't good, just that I didn't own my own life once I pulled the gun on that man. So working until sweat dripped down my face and my body ached made me feel as if somehow I was standing up on my own. There were two or three shifts in the kitchen: three a.m., eight a.m. or afternoon. They had me washing pots and pans in water that would burn the skin off a raccoon. I hated that shit and the mornings when I didn't have to get up I lay in the bed listening to the Norfolk radio station.

This was January. On New Year's the entire wing spent twenty minutes banging on the doors. The hall rocked and shook with shouts, but no matter how hard we banged, the cell doors would not open. So we went to sleep, our arms and voices spent but the frustration still there. I went to prison for ten dollars and two hours of joyriding. I had been telling myself that I was getting back at the white man, sticking the pistol in his face like that. But I knew that was just something I told myself to get by and getting by wasn't good enough. I needed to figure out what was going on in my head and in a world where I couldn't find a place for myself without crime and violence.

Working in the kitchen helped. While I washed the pots and pans with Marcel we'd talk. He grew up in Norfolk and spent his days in the kitchen telling me about it. He had this thing he'd say, "Everybody in here from Norfolk lying about who they is—we acting like we cool when most of us hated each other. Niggas be trying to rob you for breathing two years ago want to get some chips from you now." Behind us worked the bake crew and the cooks. The runners, who cleaned off the tables as the inmates finished eating, usually spent most of the time before meals up front with the servers folding up silverware. After I'd do half of the pots and pans, I'd spend the rest of the morning with Brandon talking about the days we were missing and what happened before we'd begun to call Waverly, Virginia, home. Then, if the supervisor was gone we'd spend the day lost in spades tournaments or dining room football games. For a time it was cool. I couldn't get along with Mr. Bates, the supervisor. He had one of those heads so big he had to get a special baseball cap for it. He was always on me about something. On everyone really, but at the time I wanted to believe he was just fucking with me, as if he came to work thinking, "I'm going to get that Betts today." And even though I didn't want to give him a reason to fire me, I always found reasons to be in his face arguing with him. Most days I either wouldn't sweep or take out the trash and couldn't see how the conflict began with me. I was seventeen, immature in a lot of ways and counting down my sentence from 3,285 days.

Some mornings on the line I gave everyone I knew something extra. A lot of us did that. We'd balance it out by shaking the spoon on the people we didn't know or didn't like. They'd come in and instead of getting two full spoons or spoon and a half of oatmeal, they'd get half a spoon. They'd get two sausages instead of three or a waffle and a half instead two. Worst that could happen was the person complained and someone made you give them more food. They weren't going to put their hands on you, at least that's what folks thought. Otherwise we would have given them what everyone else got.

I worked for weeks before getting fired. Mr. Bates wanted me to clean a table again, and I didn't want to. The tables were silver and I could see the light bouncing back at me as I stared at it. I walked out of the cafeteria, told him, "I forgot something in the cell, I'll do that shit when I get back." I knew if I walked out of the kitchen I was going to get fired. I had to do the time, but didn't have to be treated any kind of way for twenty cents an hour. I would miss the extra food, the break from the cell's monotony—but I wasn't too much for following orders that didn't make sense. I told myself I didn't want to work there anyway, said it was slaving to work for twenty cents an hour.

In the kitchen is where I started drifting the way of the Five Percenters. The Five Percenters believed they were god, and that anyone looking toward a being in the sky to bring them peace was deluding themselves. I thought they knew the secret to leaving these walls with something you couldn't get anywhere else. It wasn't a religion, and it wasn't about depending on what you couldn't see or waiting for some salvation after the body became dirt again. It was a different soundscape altogether. After having stood before a judge, after having been ushered through a system that was white on one side and black on the other—I was ready to draw my own color lines. And so I let the world be split in half: on one side the white man was the devil, and on the other side the black man was god. At night I thought to myself, if only the gods running around this prison could find a way to split walls wide open and stop our mothers, sisters and daughters from crying we'd be on to something.

Back on A wing, half a dozen young boys could be heard every day going over *today's mathematics*. There was Wise, Divine, Absolut, Righteous, Born and Star. They spent their days spelling out the Bible's contradictions and breaking down the exegesis of the teachings of men whose names I'd never heard before. What they spoke was a splash of black power and the Nation of Islam's nationalist rhetoric, and so what if we were hearing it thirty years late, if by the time we reached those cells most of what we heard was either dated or discredited. I thought it gave them the straightness I saw in their backs. For the first time in my life young men who could remember posting up on a block, or the last blunt they smoked, gathered in groups to "do the knowledge," and that in itself was empowering. I wanted the knowledge they slung around casually and the language they spoke.

To become a part of the Nation of Gods and Earths, or Five Percenters as everyone called them, meant you had to first fast. Initially it was a three-day fast. For a seventeen-year-old, living where young men were chained to sentences that literally threatened their sanity, the Five Percenters represented a Sunday morning's calmness. Imagine, I was seventeen years old and around me a group of young boys my age spent hours discussing metaphysics and the socioeconomic issues that led to the high rates of black male incarceration. I met Born. His name was an attribute, a rejection of something his mama gave him. After I met him I began walking closer to the line of Five

Percenters, with their talk of lessons and plus degrees. That's what I wanted, because that's where I thought the knowledge was hidden. For the first time my passion to learn was enough, I didn't have to believe in anything but myself. According to the Five Percenters, each letter of the alphabet represented something else. *S* meant self-savior. It fit into what prison meant for me. I was seventeen and there was no one I could call on for help. When fights broke out, there wasn't anyone swinging for you. Self-savior sounded sacrilegious but true. I told Born I wanted to learn, that I wanted to *build*.

In less than four months I'd pitched myself into two distinct groups. One was the highly orthodox Muslims, the other the Nation of Gods and Earths. I was seventeen and had no real clue about the way the world was moving around me. Just about everyone was still in the middle of some last-ditch appeal.

After I started talking with Born, Divine and a couple of other cats, I finally figured out that the Five Percent nation was born out of the Nation of Islam. It took those talks with Born and the others for me to learn that the earth was made up of three kinds of people: eighty-five percent of the people were deaf, dumb and blind to what was really going on; ten percent knew the truth, but either hid it or profited from it; and Five Percenters who were the poor righteous teachers. If this didn't make sense anywhere else in the world it made sense to me. Locked in a prison cell most of the time where prospects of a future or dreams were buried in the slim to none chances of getting an appeal and the lessons were trying to teach me something. It doesn't matter that I didn't get it, that I couldn't get with all the procedures. To really become a member, you had to be someone's seed. You had to get up under their wing and learn what it meant to be god-body. I wasn't ready to follow anyone, so my inclusion was always shaky. Some people thought I was just trying to steal knowledge. And maybe I was, but the reality is that all of us were there trying to raise ourselves.

'd been out of the kitchen for a few weeks and was hardly ever seeing Brandon. On any given day we were no more than a hundred, two hundred feet away from each other, but we were rarely close enough to speak. When we did talk we never could forget that we were staring at the next decade in prison. The world we knew was closing its eyes to our lives and there was nothing we could do. Knowing that is what led me to look for the math in the first place.

Part of me wanted to stay there forever, to do my bid in the relative safety of the receiving center. But not being able to move will drive you crazy. I'd been rebelling against the COs since I'd lost my job. Breaking stupid rules they set up that made no sense to me. We could buy Walkmans but couldn't buy tapes or CDs and could only get a radio station if we made an antenna out of a torn soda can. Tearing the soda can was illegal, so each morning when they walked through the cells making sure everyone was alive and no one had tried to saw the bars off at night, they took the antennas.

I spent my last month there in trouble. Small things. With the trouble came the rush to get transferred. I wanted out of the little hallway that housed us, and each morning I talked it up like I was Black. When they said the bus was coming to get someone, I'd say I was next. I was still building with the Five Percenters, and anyone who was looking at us would have considered me one. Maybe I was. I never was too sure about it. But soon it didn't matter. When it was time to go, they opened my door like they did everyone else's. The day before the move, they had us pack our stuff up and begin the twenty-four-hour wait that led to another set of shackles and ankle bracelets, that led to a van ride and another prison.

WHAT I LEARNED ABOUT CO

Correctional officers, COs for short, spent eight-hour shifts locked up with us. Some of them were beautiful, women who walked around with uniforms so tight they made you want to apologize to the last woman you held in your arms. And they could be just as vicious and spiteful as the men they walked around with. The men who were cool believed that you needed to be locked in your cell at night just like the men who were bastards. In the past they were called jailers or turnkeys. What they corrected was a mystery.

All they needed to get their job was a high school diploma or its equivalent. They would split your head to the white meat if needed. The old men who had become lieutenants and majors had spent just as much time inside the walls of prisons as men with life sentences. Their uniforms are provided by the state just like the inmates. Spending that much time in prison does something to you. Every CO is trained in lethal weapons. The black COs always reminded me that count times and chow calls didn't define my life.

[21]

Another Trip in the Wrong Direction

Tuesday morning in March of 1997 found me shackled, hand-cuffed and sitting dim-eyed in what anywhere else would be a family van. I was with five other cats: Absolut, Shorty, Clay, white boy Steve and Clarence. We waited for the short ride to the Southampton Correctional Center, a prison in the southeastern part of Virginia. Anyone would have called us motley. And if there is a face that a convict owns, that a man on his way to prison sports like a do-rag, none of us had it. Not one of us looked like we belonged on that bus, on that particular day. Me, Steve and Shorty had hints of a beard touching our jawlines. Steve trimmed the little facial hair he had so that a pencil-thin line traced the edge of his face from ear to ear. It didn't make him look older though, it just gave him a sharp line tracing his jaw. Everyone else was barefaced. The six of us could have been on a school field trip or members of a Scared Straight program, and sure as my moms was at home somewhere crying, wasn't any one of us old enough to legally smoke or buy liquor.

When we got to the prison it was the same game as the jail and the receiving center. A walk through the gates headed us straight for intake, except this time there was no need for the lice bath. At intake we peeled off our blue jumpsuits and the young guard inspected our naked bodies. After being strip-searched, I dressed in the first pair of jeans I'd worn since my arrest. It took a second for me to be staring into a camera, imagining it was my driver's license picture. The picture was pasted over a small box on the yellow ID card whose color let the guards know we were all under eighteen.

I'd never been to college, but when I walked on the yard, the first thing I thought of was a college campus with the buildings framing a courtyard where a few trees and a single bench sit. There was nothing of *American Me*, from where I stood. Nothing of the ice picks and fistfights that they say flood a prison with noise and pain. There also weren't any other inmates in sight. Just the six of us walking across an empty courtyard. Even when we got to the infirmary and walked through the door with peeling white paint and cracked wood, we were nearly alone. A guard put us in a holding cage to await our names. The room smelled of coffee and cigarette smoke. A nurse came by to tell us the rules. Her litany was a long no: "Don't borrow anything. No cigarettes, no food. You'll be all right."

When we walked outside I knew God had drawn a shade over the bright March sun. A black guard working in the property room, chomping a wad of chewing tobacco that dripped red spit on everything he handed me to sign, gave me the black bag that I dragged behind me from the property office. It held all my possessions: two sets of crisp white sheets, a blanket and a pillow, three pairs of white boxers, three pairs of white socks and three sets of state blues (denim jeans, blue dress shirts). In the bag were also a Bible and the large first volume of W.E.B. Dubois's collected works. As it scraped the concrete, I hoped it wouldn't burst open and spill my life on the sidewalk.

Six of us arrived there that Tuesday morning. Don't nobody like Tuesdays. They ain't Mondays but they're still early enough to leave room for what could be a bad week. Did I say none of us was old enough to smoke, drink or flip through pages of pornography that became staple reading at the jail? One boy wasn't even old enough to get a learner's permit in Maryland.

From anywhere on the courtyard you could see a fence wired with steel that would cut a man thinking he could jump to freedom. I'd be lying if I said I wasn't thinking about jumping. Who wouldn't be? With nine years on my back, a jump over the fence, if I thought I could get away with it, would have been the next best thing to breathing. None of us talked; it was like walking across the yard snatched our breath. Ten minutes before, when the guard walking us said that we were being put in cells together, it made me calm. One less thing to worry about. The guard said, "All of you are going to C-three." He laughed. "The prison's on lockdown." Lockdown. No one told us what that meant, but we all knew it was the reason why we'd been walking around an empty prison for an hour. Someone got stabbed.

Inside C3 it was night. As we walked in, a pair of blue denim state jeans fluttered afire like an orange butterfly, until the pool of water collecting in front of the cells on the far end of the tier extinguished it. My first day in prison and we walked into the tail end of a riot. Every guard in the building had on a black raincoat and a hat. The food carts sat filled with hot trays near the front of the building. A guard attempting to pass out the food was nearly struck with a can of Sprite. He avoided the can coming at his head like a right jab, and then pivoted around looking for the face of the thrower. Nearly every cell on the tier had a man gaping through bars laughing at the guard's rage.

The noise was another kind of riot. It brushed up against the decay of the building. Drab. Harsh. Surreal. The noise blew out from cells and blended curses into something that no one could fully decipher. "CO, I wish the can . . . Your mother . . . Rich, send me a . . ." It was all mumbo jumbo by the time it reached our ears, and when the guard pushed the door closed behind me it was less than that. With the screaming outside the door as the backdrop, the CO led me and Steve to a cell that was so small we could barely move around. It contained nothing but a bunk bed with two threadbare mattresses and two small lockers. Steve tossed his bag on the bottom bunk as a way of claiming it. Bottom bunk some type of treat, like it was going to make a cell less of a cell. When I went to sit down, Steve asked, "What you think we need to do to keep the water from getting in here?"

I'd forgotten about the water and when I walked to the cell door I could hear the guards swishing around. "It ain't really flowing like that down this end. Let's wait and see."

Southampton, this dark, dark hole we'd just been ushered into, is often called the Farm, because years ago inmates farmed the grounds, planting and harvesting whatever would grow in that dirt. Many of us knew that arriving at the prison was the end and that after the first night our days would fall into an unpredictable monotony. Steve had thirty-five years. What else was there for him? He was seventeen then, sixteen when he got locked up.

"Yo, Shy? A yo, Shy Boogie?" I heard somebody calling me from the other building. It was Rashid's voice. He'd been transferred to the Farm a few days before me. At the receiving center Rashid sounded like Buju Banton as he chanted, "Murderer, Blood is on your shoulder" with nothing but his closed fist beating against a cell door for a rhythm. He turned some nights on A wing into a reggae concert that lasted until the bustle of men yelling back and forth through cell doors quieted to only his voice in the wee hours of the morning. His voice rang out like that when chanting or saying the adhan, which let the other Muslims know it was time to pray. Rashid was in the opposite building, in the cell directly across from me. I took the chipped plastic that served as a window down and leaned out.

"Rashid, man, it's crazy over here. Fires are in the halls, we haven't eaten." I leaned so far out the window that my shoulders were outside. We didn't have a screen and I wondered if anyone had ever been desperate enough to jump. "Is it raining?"

"We gonna get us some showers today, Lieutenant," someone screamed from the cell opposite mine. I could hear the demand in his voice, as if it were showers or a trouble the lieutenant didn't want to see. The water that dripped onto my head, shirt and cell floor wasn't rain. The sun outside barely beat against the cool March air, but it wasn't raining. Above me someone had flooded their toilet. Buckets of toilet water washed down the hole around the pipe in the back corner of the cell.

Steve crouched on one knee, clogging up the hole beneath the door. "Damn, we should have blocked this door." Water flowed freely inside from the hallway. Each cell had a pipe running down the back corner that provided heat for bodies, and heated water for coffee if you tied a bag with cold liquid around the pipe with a string. Old heads and anyone with sense enough to make do with what wasn't there could turn that hot water into a morning cup of coffee before count cleared. Those pipes had gaping holes around the tops, and the men in the cells on the bottom floor, who expected people in the cells above them to flood, closed those holes with boxers, T-shirts or anything to keep water from raining down on their heads, beds and electronics. No one had told us to clog the hole up. Steve was seventeen, white and locked up in a prison cell for the first time; I was seventeen, black and locked up in a prison cell for the first time. What was either one of us going to know about stopping flood water from flowing into our cell?

"They flooding over here, too," Rashid yelled back as I started to clean my cell. I had no real idea what was going on. My life was feeling more and more like a movie. No, it was my life turning into a hundred different movies, all playing at once. There was so much going on that no one person could care about all of it. Everyone thought they were the star of the show, but the truth was all of us were blind to what happened outside the square we stood in. I thought the world revolved around me and not the white boy with the bald head who had thirty-five years. Steve thought the world rested in the secret to get him out of them years. And then there was this: my first full day in prison and I saw trash floating down the hall; the guards refuse to feed us lunch; and all around me men in cages yelling about who was going to get fucked the fuck up. The rule was that when the prison was locked down, inmates received showers every seventy-two hours. When I arrived, the prison had been on lock for four days with no showers and no phone calls. The flooding and fires was the response.

That night we got showers. We got showers and were able to use the telephones before they told us to return to our cells.

Rumor had more stories about the start of the fight that led to the stabbing than I have time to tell. The one that's stuck with me is this: two dudes, one from Norfolk and one from Richmond, got to arguing about Tupac and Biggie. Fists followed, and then a slender piece of metal sharpened to a point went into somebody's shoulder. It made no sense, but it makes perfect sense. Tupac's *Makaveli* was the last tape I listened to before a Sunday morning ended with my slender wrists in handcuffs. The tape I slid into the forest green Grand Prix I'd decided looked better with me behind the wheel than the sleeping white man for no better reason than the pistol that caused my palm to sweat. A month went by and the fights that broke out were over something, or they were over nothing, but they were never so important that the reasons for the fight or even the story of the fight itself persisted. What I thought was a riot wasn't even a real riot. A hiccup at best, the COs never really tripping about the fire and flooding because they didn't sleep in the buildings with us and all the cell doors were locked. All that happened was I got wet on my first day there, and the building got showers and phone calls. Nobody went home early.

None of us were forming ourselves into the kind of close-knit groups I saw at the reception center. And that was fine with me, because whatever truth I had was slipping through my hands every day, and I'd long been questioning whether anything I found in prison could change my life.

Mornings, Wise walked out of his cell and said, "What's the science, God?" I answered. At the receiving center the Five Percenters looked like young militants, all standing with their arms folded over their chests. It wasn't like that there. But ask anybody and they'll tell you I was right there: yelling out the days in the divine alphabet, breaking it down, too. But by then my memory had faded. I wasn't studying every day, because I had started thinking the loose-leaf paper that someone had written the lessons on didn't hold the secret to the universe the way I'd thought it would.

"Sun, what's the science?" It wasn't always a question. Sometimes it was more like a "what's up." Wise was lighting up a Black and Mild. We'd smoked it on the way to breakfast, passing it back and forth like it was a blunt and we were getting high, but we weren't. We were stealing seconds away from the cells and hiding them in the peace of smoke rebelling against gravity as it drifted from our lungs. We'd found the teachings of Elijah Muhammad and the Nation of Islam about thirty years too late and so what if our revolution was nothing more than sharing all we had with each other. All of us. The small group of young brothers I rolled with at the receiving center and the folks I knew at the Farm. We shared what we had, bonded in a makeshift way by what we'd inherited. So what if it hadn't sparked the revolution it was supposed to, or if the weight of the earth was never going to get a man out of prison a second earlier. It had to be okay, 'cause it kept some of us sane, while it drove some of us mad. Or that's what I'd begun to think. I was still going by the name Shahid. And I'd say I was fronting except there was this sincerity in what led me to look for the name. And taking the name was different from believing that the black man was God; it was different from me proving that the white man was the devil, too.

22

Weed

didn't believe I'd get high. We wanted to make a part of prison resemble home, so some of us waxed our cell floors. We hung up pictures on cell walls. Watched reruns of *Martin*. We smoked weed.

Newports cost one dollar and eighty-five cents per pack. I didn't smoke but knew the cost because Newports were currency. Each week when I went to the commissary and filled up an orange bag with Cheetos and noodles, I also grabbed some blows. That's what we called them in there: blows. *Blows*, just like money behind the walls where a dollar bought contraband charges. The yellow plastic ID card in my pocket was supposed to mean that I couldn't buy a pack. But the women working commissary, black and white, always gave me what I was willing to pay for. They must have seen the rule for what it was: bullshit. Why couldn't I buy tobacco? Because I was seventeen? I was locked up in the dusted and worn cells just like any grown man, doing my time in the same place he did, so why couldn't I buy a pack of Newports like everyone else?

WEED   [143]

I say the women at the counter understood what it was to get locked in a cell at night without a single cigarette, or to have to ask, borrow or buy tobacco to support an addiction you came to prison with. They might have just liked me. I was respectful and said hi when I walked up. I flirted with them. Most commissary days Steve wanted me to buy him a crate of Blacks and a box of Newports, but I hated walking around with a lot of stuff in my commissary bag. I was paranoid thinking the bag full of food made me a target. But if walking around with a little food and cigarettes made me a target, walking around with nothing would make me a target, too, especially if I was going hungry out of fear. So I bought the stuff. Steve would stare at my list trying to figure out what combination of snacks and hygiene I'd penciled in would add up to the thirty-dollar cost of the crate of Blacks and box of Newports.

"Shy, if you buy the shit, I'll get all your food this week. You know they're not going to let me get nothing. I don't know why the fuck you always come back here with shit, like your ID card ain't yellow. But I need some blows this week. I told Chris that I wanted to get some weed from him. It's three packs for a J. You want in? I'll pay the two since you buying my blows for me."

I hadn't been high since two days before the steel cuffs clanked over my wrists the first time. Steve was freaking a Black and Mild, waiting for me to answer. I said I wasn't getting high anymore, but I didn't really think about it before I responded, "Aiight, I'm in." Steve was the only white boy there I rapped with, and I only talked to him 'cause he was in the cell with me. He walked around with thirty-five years on his back because he shot somebody in the face after a beef at a party. All his co-defendants were black, and doing about as much time as he was. If I couldn't explain the shit I did to my moms, I knew he had no hope of explaining killing someone over an argument at a party. We never talked about time. Never. There was nothing to say about knowing you're going to spend the rest of your good years in here. Thinking about it made me want to get high.

"We gonna wait until lock to smoke? Till when the CO's gonna be doing rounds. Young, you ever looked at the little Italian chick work our floor?"

I knew who he was talking about but couldn't remember her name. She had a mud face though. Acted like she was cute because whenever she came on the tier ten people were up in her face. I didn't say much to her. Tried to stay out of the way. The Italian woman once saw me hiding in the TV room after our tier came inside from rec. They let the tiers out one at a time. Usually we alternated and got to go out either in the morning and after dinner or just once after lunch. You could get around this if you hid somewhere. We called it beating rec. Smith was her name. She saw me creep into the TV room when I should have been going to my cell. She told the CO in the booth to open my door anyway. When she saw me step into the TV room she knew I was beating rec. A cell door open for longer than it takes you to walk to it was an invitation to be robbed. She knew that, but knew I couldn't say, "Why you open my cell when I was about to beat rec?" I was thinking about all that when the CO announced count time. "Yeah, what about her?"

"I think she got something for me. You think she'd take me in the back room?"

This was the prisoner's dream. Meet a halfway decent-looking woman who works in the system and have sex with her. She could be a CO, a secretary, kitchen supervisor—as long as she was willing to lead you to a place where no one could see and open her legs. I knew Steve was going to say something like that. Every morning he lined up the little piece of beard he had on his face. With thirty-five years though, the only hope he had of touching a woman was if one of those COs went for him. We'd only been there a minute and I knew the stories. I told him he was crazy. She was in everyone's face.

Doing her time off the looks and attention men with thirty, forty, fifty years gave her.

"Here it is."

"Here what is?" He had this little-ass white stick in his hand. No thicker than it would be if it were rolled up with air, and I knew he wasn't telling me my pack of Newports bought that. Even if there was weed inside the paper, it was less than what I'd have thrown away after rolling up a blunt. "You not about to tell me this is what I paid for."

"Nah, Shy, I'm telling you, we both gonna be high in a minute."

He lit the J, and it smelled like weed all right. It had been a minute but you don't forget the smell. I hadn't been looking for weed 'cause I hadn't been looking for habits, but it had been awhile and I was tired of staring at those walls. When he passed it to me, I pulled and felt the smoke hit my chest. It was gone in a minute or two and I knew I wasn't high. "Can't no dust, no straps that you throw on the floor get me high."

I heard Steve on the bottom bunk laughing. It doesn't take long to know you're high. It snuck up on me and pulled my eyelids closed. The weed made me remember what it was like to lean against a fence off of Silver Hill Road, close my eyes and pull so hard the smoke made me cough. "You right. I'm high as gas," I told Steve and thought that Chris must have made cartons of Newports on a nickel bag of weed. In Southampton, the business of selling weed was more lucrative than it would ever be on the streets. Maybe my numbers were off, but he'd make fifty to a hundred dollars off of a nickle bag easy.

found the library two days later. It was tucked into a small area and was halfway decent. On the humble I picked up a Russian novel about a Russian prison. The men there didn't have cellmates and the walls were so thick they couldn't talk through them. They had to devise a Morse code: a way of banging on the wall that conveyed letters and words and sentences. If prison is nothing else it is where you learn to take what you have and fashion what you need. There were men who made tattoo guns out of the motors in Walkmans, men who made ink out of smoke. I watched people walk in cells only to come out hours later with their backs and arms turned into canvases that told the world there was still something in the world worth remembering every day besides the inside of a prison cell. Sometimes it was an RIP, sometimes it was a child's name, but it was always something that someone thought was important enough to look at as often as they had to look at the bars on the prison cell.

Everyone at Southampton thought Steve was trying to be black. His head had been bald since I met him and his jeans hung lower than most. His photo album was filled with pretty young black girls and black dudes with the names of neighborhoods on their T-shirts. Even his stories and his use of the term *young* instead of *stickman* or *blood* or *sun* or *peace god*, all of it said he was just like the rest of us black boys, even down to his sentence, thirty-five years for a boy with nothing to shave. Because he suffered like the rest of us and would fight without thinking, most people just accepted him as white boy Steve.

23

The People I Knew

learned that you could buy hot water. In solitary confinement at Fairfax I read Max Weber's *The Protestant Work Ethic and the Spirit of Capitalism*. They'd put me in the hole for assaulting a guard. A deputy had come to tell me I was being moved to another block. We were standing in the hallway and he reached to close my door, and he signaled I was going to the hole if I didn't move. I grabbed his arm and I started to say, nah, I'll move . . . but he'd slammed me against the wall as soon as I touched him. I talk with my hands, tapping people on the arm and shoulder when I want their attention. I didn't realize that was assault and would land me in the hole for ten days. It helped me in the long run, though. While I was in the hole, Ms. Elman sent me a stack of books: Dickens's *Great Expectations* and *Oliver Twist*, some Faulkner and Weber's book. I wasn't but sixteen then and couldn't understand what Weber was saying about capitalism. I looked around me now and knew there was no Protestant work ethic that fueled capitalism there. It was all hunger and imagination. No ovens, microwaves or hot water heaters available to inmates, so some inmate had figured out a way to run electricity through water. A white boy named Tommy in a cell near the front of the tier ran a business where he'd heat a cup of water for you for a soup. Fifteen cents is what it cost.

Prison was split into a number of little worlds and since no one in my world knew Tommy, I was lucky to meet him. The Virginia system had a history of beef between people from D.C. and those from down South. I had never been one to draw regional lines, but sometimes they drew themselves. When we weren't in groups based on religion or sports, we were in groups based on region. Afternoons I'd walk to the chow hall with Wise and then we'd split as he sat with his folks from Norfolk and I sat wherever I could fit in. I also knew I'd peel off. Sit in a circle with too many people I didn't know and the attention was bound to turn to me, somebody would try his hand at being a comedian and that would lead to somebody getting punched in the mouth. I was trying to walk around invisible, but I soon learned that there was no invisible in prison.

There was an unspoken rule that if you were from D.C. or northern Virginia or Maryland, nine times out of ten you'd hang with each other. You'd walk the yard together, eat together, and if anyone fucked with somebody in the group, if something ever jumped off, you'd throw punches together. There wasn't the gang violence like on Discovery Channel specials about prison. It was just random collections of people who hung together because they shared the same slang, the same memory of cities and streets in their head or the same way of life.

Sometimes groups overlapped. A guy from Richmond might run with the Muslims or the Five Percenters or the Christians or the ballplayers, and sometimes people ran together 'cause they were all thieves or they were all homosexuals. *Ran together*, another way of saying treating folks like family—because sometimes they were the only family you had. It meant that you could eat at the time and not have it eat at you, losing yourself in moments when you found peace shooting hoops, playing chess or walking around the track talking about the color shorts Yolanda had on the first time you saw her at the pool. We needed those moments.

It was Norfolk, Richmond, Portsmouth and Newport News down there. No one from the city or anywhere close to it was close enough to home for our families to see the prison every day on their way to work or school, but folks from the Tidewater and Richmond areas were close enough to get visits each weekend. In the chow hall you could hear the stories ringing back and forth at each table. Young brothers and old heads trading stories about when they ran the streets. It was the same with Richmond, Portsmouth and Newport News. D.C., too. Anywhere you found three, four dudes from the same area you were going to hear stories about home. What the stories were about was less important than the telling, 'cause no matter what, the telling of the stories took everyone away from this dirt and grass and concrete of the Farm.

Steve was from northern Virginia, Woodbridge somewhere, same place my grandma was from. Leaf, Lil Ron, Cliff all were from northern Virginia somewhere. I would catch them on the yard and hear their stories. Their slang was what I grew up hearing, even if the streets they remember never felt my feet. Leaf's little brother was locked up with me at Landmark, the youngest littlest dude in there. His mouth was bigger than mine and he wasn't but ten or eleven. That's how it was, get picked up for truancy or a fight and the next thing you knew half the people you were tight with were locked up or had been locked up. Rob somebody or shoot somebody and everybody you were tight with was locked up.

The people I knew couldn't keep drama from coming my direction. And when the drama came it didn't matter where you were from. It was simply about how fast you threw your fists, or if you threw them at all. Truth is it took two months for me to get punched in the face. What if every story I tell about this place is a map that leads you to the way shackles and cuffs lock around wrists and minds, that leads you to the ways men are left with nothing to embrace but the insanity of a well-placed jab. The punch left my jaw aching and my lip split. My knuckles were fine though. Didn't throw one punch. Was walking to the shower with the rubber shower shoes they sell at canteen on my feet. In my naïveté, I didn't know it made more sense to go to the shower with your boots. Walking down the hall you heard it all, lies kicking back off the bars and TVs yelling sports scores, playing cards slammed on the metallic tables. It all thinly veiled the violence of a cat waking up to a bad day, but there was something about those times that left me feeling like I could live above the fray.

He bumped me, right when my feet stepped in the puddle of water by the utility closet, just a few feet from the shower. What I care that he bumped into me? It wasn't a hard bump, wasn't an "I'm 'bout to punch you in the face" bump.

"Damn, watch yourself." That's what I said. Open showers. No curtains to separate one from the other, just a little piece of brick that was maybe six inches high was all you had to step over to get from one shower to the next. I usually took my showers in the morning when there were fewer people there. Sometimes it was so crowded we did the pick and roll in the shower. Eight naked men using three or four showers, taking a few seconds to get wet, then soaping up while someone else got wet, then sliding back in to rinse off. After rec, when bodies lined up like cars awaiting repair, getting clean was to put yourself on an assembly line and move in circles, getting wet in one stall, then soaping up in the next as men crowded the space around you. The shower was near the front of the tier, right by the booth.

"Damn, watch yourself." Then he was swinging. I can tell you I weaved the first punch, and then slipped in the water. The second punch grazed my nose but split my lip, the others connected with the air in the space where my face was before I'd fallen in the little puddle. Two months in and my lip was swollen and I didn't hit him back 'cause I froze for a second before I got up and when I unfroze the COs were putting me in cuffs, taking me to a cell near the other end of the tier. Or maybe I didn't swing back because I was frightened. The prison bloomed a world where every breath created a reason to hit someone in the mouth, to be hit in the mouth—and I forgot that long enough to find myself rubbing a sore jaw.

The single cell in the back of the building was *a* hole but not *the* hole. It was one of the five or six cells they used to keep prisoners in what the COs called pretrial detention whenever one of us caught a series institutional charge. There were rules in prison that covered everything, and if you broke those rules there were charges. Every charge was coded by a number and laid out in a little yellow book: a 105 was an assault, 210 was disobeying a direct order. There were other charges for contraband, charges for fighting. When charges carried time in the hole, you were placed on prehearing detention. It was just like getting locked up before your court date and being denied bond. What it meant was that after the fight the COs locked me in a single cell at the end of the tier and I could do nothing but contemplate fucking up the light-skinned kid whose name I didn't know. His swinging and my falling formed the tragicomic entertainment for one night. Everybody saw him steal on me. If I didn't do anything about it, somebody would think they could take my shoes, steal whatever was in my cell. Or fuck me.

"What you gonna do, Shahid?" Shorty's eyes floating a question into my cell. The good thing about still being on the tier was that I could talk to people; the bad thing was that the people I talked to always wanted to know what I was going to do about what happened.

"I'll take care of it when I get out." No one cared what I did. They just wanted to see the drama. Everyone wanted to see something jump off. And the truth is you don't think about time until it starts to get heavy. Right then time started getting heavy and the years felt like a noose around my neck.

Steve never came to see me, but Wise, who had over thirty years too, came by and he told me the happenings on the yard. "The kid who tagged you is a Muslim, one of Rashid's brothers. I don't know what's up with him, but we can find out when you get out of here." I didn't pay too much attention to what folks said to me, but I figured Wise wasn't looking for entertainment.

The other young dudes that walked to my cell door all wanted to know what really happened. Did I get two-pieced and drop hard against the floor like a gavel or was it really one straight shot to the nose before my eyes closed and head slammed against the wall? In that cell I reflected on the books I'd been reading. Being at the Farm meant I had access to all the books and information about the Nation of Islam, Five Percenters and Islam that I wanted. *The Willie Lynch Letter, The Destruction of Black Civilization, Theology of Time, Behold a Pale Horse, Mentacide.* Books that were about Islam and about black folks in general. We were living in a world governed by the rage of a bloody knife and at some point, no matter what I did to the young brother who swung on me once I got out the hole, I had to ask myself if I'd get meaning from the punches I threw or the pages I turned. I never was a fighter, so finding solace and strength in the sound of a turning page seemed the move. The problem was I had to live in population. I wasn't ever going to be the person who checked into protective custody because I couldn't defend myself. I had no idea what I'd do when they let me off lock, but knew if it came down to it I'd throw a right to his head before talking.

I'd told people to call me Shahid. If you asked them what the name meant literally, maybe they couldn't tell you. Shahid: Arabic for the witness. It was strange wanting to be a witness in a place no one cares about. The idea of writing made me think about witnessing. What else was Walter Mosley doing in all of his Easy stories but writing about a man who was both detective and witness. My mom wrote letters asking me how I was doing, asking me if I was safe. I couldn't tell her how it was in there, couldn't tell her how many young boys were in there hurting from what they did and from what others did to them. Hurting from what the courts did every time they sent a young man to a place governed by fists and randomness. I figured if people called me Shahid because I told them to, I could be a witness and say something about what it means to run headfirst into what you always wanted to avoid. In there having never fired a pistol, never stomped anyone out, never posed for a driver's license picture, never gone to a prom, never having done much of anything but play with the line between trouble and straight—I couldn't help but feel like I was witnessing a life I was supposed to avoid. All my life my teachers had told me being labeled talented and gifted and attending magnet schools made me somehow smarter, better than the boys around me. Yet we were all there together. The name Shahid was how I understood what it meant to have the two worlds I lived in as a child slam together and fit neatly in a prison cell. I was still seventeen; still remembered that I'd never talked about one book I'd read with my friends until a cell door closed behind me. So if I say where else could I find black teenagers huddled together building on the relative importance of the first verse of Pac's "White Man's World" one moment and Elijah Muhammad's theology the next, I already know there's no place like this I know. Scholarship brushing up against black militancy brushing up against pseudoscience brushing up against the rage we carried within us brushing up against the years that got stacked up on our heads, that's what I saw daily. And since I'm thinking about it, I'm fulfilling my own prayer: Shahid, to be a witness, and tell somebody what a cell does to men and juveniles both.

hear this story in my ears and it sounds so neat. That's what I did in the hole that first time: told stories to myself to patch up the holes in the drama that had me on the wrong end of a nine-year sentence. I kept my eyes closed to the minutiae and the drama of life in prison when I wrote my family letters. I told them about the weather, not about the hole and definitely not how I stopped using my father's name. There wasn't a language that was going to make what was happening make sense to them.

Some things I can't tell anyone, pieces of the story that get left out as I go along. Southampton was four hours from anyone I knew. When I walked the yard, it was never with someone I went to school with, someone I grew up with. That made me an outsider even when I was with Leaf and them. There was this old head from Suitland. Everyone I knew called him Davis, and honestly I don't know if that was his first name or his last. He got locked up in '82. That meant he missed *Beat Street* and *Purple Rain*. He probably didn't see *Cooley High* when it came out in '75 since he wasn't but fifteen when he got locked up. He missed crack and the eighties that drove my daddy's generation crazy. I talked to him, but what was he going to tell me when he hadn't seen the streets since I was a little baby. His whole life was trapped in those cells—a juvenile certified as an adult before they had a name for sending kids to prison. He was the one who told me the ratio of black men, he called them bloods, to the white men in prison. Told me it was around seventy percent black. He didn't tell me about the pain that came with being in prison for sixteen years. More time in prison than he'd been free. He didn't have to tell me.

It was another type of burden for the old head. Not being from around there must have made his early days difficult. Not a soul around to remember the street he grew up on or the last girl he had a crush on. I knew brothers in there with each other, cousins. If you

were from the area, you might be walking around the field and see
the dude that got your little sister pregnant or someone who gradu-
ated from high school with you. The ties so thick and deep that in
a fucked-up way this shit almost felt natural, an extension of running wild in the streets. In Maryland they have the same prisons,
filled with brown-skinned brothers I may or may not know, but
who would recognize the names of the streets I talk about. Dudes
who would know the bands I listened to and the schools I attended.
I wouldn't be an outsider there, wouldn't need an *in* to connect with
the people I was doing time around: it wouldn't matter if I played
ball, if I was a Muslim, a Five Percenter or what have you because
I'd have bonds with someone that went back to a shared history; but
there, figuring out who I could let play me close was like cupping
dice in my palms, knowing the falling dice would show a hot hand
or snake eyes.

24

The Cost of a Knife

knife costs a carton of Newports. I was only on lockdown for a week and when I got out, it was like that information was looking for me. I was in cell four, right by the booth in the front, with a cellie from Richmond with a sentence that was more than our ages combined plus ten. A middle linebacker's number: sixty-two years. And since parole had been abolished in Virginia that was as good as a life sentence. Two days in the cell with him and I'd been thinking about his time more than his name. When I first learned I had to do eighty-five percent of my time it crushed me, but I knew I could do eighty-five percent of nine years. Eighty-five percent of sixty-two years was the sound of somebody's mother crying forever. I been thinking about his sixty years and the cost of a knife all night and now it is morning.

It took two weeks in a cell to learn someone's entire life and tell yours. After that two weeks, you're just filling in details that color how you got to where you are: in a cell in the southern part of Virginia. Every morning, a couple of minutes before it was time for breakfast, the CO in the booth opened all the doors on the tier. I was always up before the door opened. Breakfast was the best meal in here and anyway I didn't like the idea of the door opening with me in the bed asleep. I never could get away from the stories I'd heard. Stories of people getting bum rushed when the doors opened, or having their doors rigged shut as somebody set the cell on fire. Most of the stories were from other prisons and other times. Places where to come to prison was to enter into a dice game with the devil for your life not just your sanity. Roger never cared. He never went to breakfast, so I didn't wake him. Roger's photo album was still on the dresser when I jumped off the bunk. I noticed the picture of his daughter in the album. She was just a baby in it, not even a month old. He told me she was born while he was at the jail. His birthday was two months before mine, same year. Been locked up the same amount of time. That morning I walked to the chow hall alone, thinking about what the little girl in the picture would have to pay before it's all over with.

One afternoon Roger was at the cell door with his boys from Richmond. Their gold and silver teeth gleamed while one of them freaked a Black and Mild. Sometime before I watched him pull the head of the straw broom off of its stick and now he's slipping the stick down his pants leg. He told me he'd do something to the first person jumped out of line. The stick was free, comes with the broom they put in each cell. The knife cost a carton of Newports. I could have just beat the dude that hit me over the head with a stick for free; except beat him over the head or stab him and any judge in Virginia adds five to ten years to my sentence, plus the nine years the judge suspended.

When I got out the hole I didn't do anything to the dude. I wasn't mad enough, that's all. When I walked into the courtroom the judge listened as the prosecutor called me a menace to society. I hadn't been in a fight since about the sixth grade. Hadn't won a fight since the fourth. The night of the robbery was my first time holding a gun, and there I was in prison walking away when it could make people think I was soft. I didn't want to fight and wasn't afraid or mad enough to just start swinging. I got lucky. I didn't have to pay for it. I watched others rumble as if their lives depended on it and still get burned, come away with one less pair of shoes, with a man thinking everything they bought belonged to him. And there were never rules to choosing who would survive and who wouldn't. Almost like it was the luck of the draw, some made it and some didn't, if you consider not making it meaning going crazy, or losing a sense of yourself. If it means when you don't care anymore, and will do anything to get over on anybody.

And the truth was there were always little reasons to care. One day I was standing in the property room picking up a book I'd bought. A dude stood in line in front of me reading a book in Spanish. I didn't ask him his name, just if he was Hispanic. He told me no. Told me that he'd taught himself. It was like walking into a little miracle. Even though every day I was seeing things that I wouldn't write home about, things that weren't inspiring me in any way, there were moments that made me pause. This young black dude had taught himself Spanish because he wanted to learn. I found those moments when I walked to the rec yard or to the cafeteria. They were few and far between but I found them.

25

Fishing from the Hole

or months I watched as every day the van brought new people. Southampton was the dumping ground for young inmates, and it seemed like there was a never-ending run of black boys walking into its halls. What that meant was that around me there were the young ones, like myself, who had just come in and the old heads who'd been in so long that prison was more home than anywhere else. I could name the old heads: Dred, Davis, Scott, the white man who did the laundry. The crazy dude who worked out like a maniac and smiled just a little too much. They represented the range of things prison could do.

When Born got to the Farm, we spent most of our time on the rec yard walking around the building. There was a trio of older brothers we talked to every day. One was Muslim, one was Rastafarian and the other was Christian. It was the first time I'd spent any considerable amount of time talking to grown men. They weren't on any of the penitentiary bullshit, but they had the scars from dealing with it. Jackson, the Christian, had been a captain of the Nation of

Islam. He'd turned his back on one set of beliefs for something he believed in more. Something that made the three life sentences he had to do manageable. Salaam, his roommate, was the imam for the compound—imam being the Islamic religious leader. And Dred, he was really the spiritual leader of the young brothers who wanted to be Rasta. All of these old heads had done twenty years, at least. I was lucky to get to be around them, to sit with them, to listen to their stories.

It was the first time I'd sat with men my father's age and learned about life. Jackson had set up his own self-help program. He's the one who told me you take what you have to get what you need, and then take what you need to get what you want. It was the first time I'd heard that, and it's stuck with me since. And what do I have to say about them? I remember Salaam. He was the only person I knew who was heated behind what had happened to Ron. Salaam was one to get mad when he saw a young boy getting handled because he couldn't handle himself. When Ron came through he wasn't but fifteen. The rumor was that he had a life sentence, but I didn't know. All I knew was that one day he was cool, running around like everyone else. The next, the whole Newport News could be seen sporting his sneakers and there was a rumor that Bear had tried to rape him. He wasn't but fifteen. Pole thin and not ready in no kind of way for what was around us. But he was light-skinned, with long hair. That made him a target for some folks. The world had gone insane. Many of the men around me called homosexuals *boys* and there were plenty of people on the lookout for someone to make theirs. One day Salaam pulled Born and me up and asked what happened to Ron. Born told him, and after that Salaam pulled Ron up under his wing. Things were what they were though, and I don't know if Ron recovered or could recover. I was in the hole again before any of it played out.

In a two-week time period Roger and I both were sent to the hole for assault on the police charges. The backdrop was Red Onion State Prison. We didn't know it at the time, but it had just opened and they needed to fill the bunks with prisoners. So the state changed its classification system so that the standards they used to assess your threat factor were more amenable to getting the beds at the Onion filled. So one year an assault charge would get you ten points, which wouldn't be enough to change your security level. Then the next year, that same assault charge got you twenty points, which guaranteed your security level was going to be raised. One morning Roger was walking to the cafeteria wearing his do-rag, the leg of a pair of long johns tied with a knot at the top. When he walked into the cafeteria a CO called out, "Let me have that contraband." Everyone around knew it was some bullshit, but Roger tossed his rag to the CO. The white man caught the hat, then called in other COs and said Roger threw the hat at him. Suddenly, tossing a hat had become an assault charge, a 105 in their rule book, and they gave Roger ninety days in segregation.

The segregation cell was in the building parallel to my cell. And lucky for Roger, he'd been put in a cell roughly across from mine. Anybody locked up for more than a few months on the Farm knew how to fish. This is when you made a line from the sheets you slept on and added some sort of hook. The hook could be a shampoo bottle full of water, a boot or a fingernail clipper. It depended on where you were sending your line. If it was going inside the building it would be a fingernail clipper or a bar of soap, but if it was going to another building it would be something heavier. Fishing was how we got stuff to each other when we were locked in the cell. At night, you could see lines drifting from the top tiers to cells on the bottom and then you'd see a laundry bag containing Black and Milds, soups or whatever the fisherman was angling for. Sometimes the bag just held a note.

With Roger across from me, we could fish. I'd attach a boot to my line and toss it halfway into the space that separated our two buildings and he'd snag it with his line. Once the lines were connected you could see a tightrope linking our two cells and you could see the pillowcase going back and forth as I sent him food and whatever else he needed. Prisoners weren't allowed to have much in the hole, so fishing was the way we supplemented and the way the segregated units and the population communicated. We could yell to each other, but that got old when you competed with seven other conversations. But our fishing didn't last long. One afternoon Born and I were coming from church with Jackson when the Italian guard told me to go to my cell. Now. In the time it took me to turn around, she was writing a charge.

It shouldn't have mattered, one charge that I would have likely beaten, but I was young and stuck on principles. I was set on going to the prison's field event. If you stayed away from trouble for a year, your family could come and walk around the prison rec yard with you for a few hours. I was especially looking forward to it because I'd heard you could have sex with someone if you were sneaky, so I was laying my plans out. While I had no one who would come up to a prison to have sex with me, I was mad that the CO was writing a charge for something so petty and ruining my chances. I tried to talk her out of the charge but couldn't. Next thing I know she was trying to slam my door in my face, but I wouldn't let her close me in the cell. The disobeying a direct order charge became an assault charge when she said I hit her with the door. Off I went to the hole with a ninety-day sentence.

People went crazy in the hole. There was no air-conditioning in the summer, so I would strip down to my boxer shorts and pour water on the bare mattress and then lie in it and wake up dry but covered with mosquito bites. There really was nothing else to do about the heat, just endure it or lie in water. The library cart didn't come around but there were plenty of people down there you could get a book from. Just like in population, inmates we called housemen cleaned up and helped pass out the food. I didn't notice them much when I was in population, but they were almost our lifelines in the hole. If not for them and fishing we wouldn't have been able to pass food, books, notes. All the stuff you needed. The housemen were in population, so they could bring word back and forth to keep that communication flowing.

I was back there on my first real charge, and honestly, I felt better in the hole; it was calm. There wasn't the pressure you feel when in population, the constant tension in the air. You disgraced yourself by "checking in"—asking to be placed in the hole for protective custody. So I'd never thought of going to the hole as a way of being able to relax. The crazy thing is, you're supposed to be safe in prison; instead, prisoners who are unwilling or unable to fight require special arrangements: checking in. I wasn't in the hole for protection, but I wasn't complaining about having a few months where all I had to worry about was what book I'd read next. In population, there were too many young dudes running around shackled to too much time and for sanity's sake my time in the hole did me good.

In the hole, once I realized I could just call out on the door for books, I was reading a book a night. Reading more and getting some time to write my thoughts out, to process what people I walked the yard with said to me. Somewhere between the receiving center and the Farm I'd stopped looking for answers in the Five Percenters or Muslims or Christians and had started being conscious of the world around me. Of prison and what that meant.

After I finished the first ninety-day stint, they gave me another. That November 5, my mother saved the money she would have spent on a birthday cake and the money she would have spent on gas to come visit me. She wasn't going to drive hours to see me shackled and cuffed behind a glass, trying my best to balance a phone between the cuffs. For my birthday I was in a cell that I only left for showers every three days and rec twice a week. For people in segregation and solitary confinement rec was in a cage that looked like a man-sized dog kennel. They put two of us in each cage and sometimes fights would break out. The cage locked so there was no escaping and fists would just be thrown as the rest of us oohed and aahed. It made us into animals, so I stopped going outside. The only time I left the cell was for showers. Two days after my birthday, I was on the door yelling for a book when someone threw *The Black Poets* by Dudley Randall under my cell door. James Baldwin said that people are trapped in history and history is trapped in them. The poets in Randall's book were telling the history in shades of gray, telling the stories I never found in schoolbooks. Everybody has a book they say has changed their life—a book that made them more than they were before they picked it up. There was something within the pages of that tiny poetry anthology that moved me.

The little anthology contained black poets from Lucy Terry to Nikki Giovanni. Robert Hayden, Etheridge Knight, Sonia Sanchez all populated that small world of poetry. It barely fit under the crack beneath my cell door. While I read Robert Hayden's "Ballad of Nat Turner" I thought about how people said the United States was a fist closed over the lives of black men. In 1831, on my birthday, Nat Turner was tried and found guilty of heading a slave revolt that led to the deaths of forty or so whites. He was sentenced to death. Hayden was expanding my history, fleshing out the story of this man who'd fought against slavery with the sharpened end of a blade. In Hayden's poem there's no mention of where the revolt took place, but rumor had it that there was a time you got sent to the hole in Southampton for saying the name Nat Turner, that the ground on which the prison was built was the same land where Turner fought for his freedom.

The book left me with what I couldn't escape. The cell door that closed on me and wouldn't open no matter how hard I yanked was first pulled shut by my own hands. And there was a history I was trapped in that I'd just begun to realize was buried in books. Books I'd read but had misunderstood because I'd never brought to my reading the desperation of a man holding a twenty-foot length of sheet that he tossed out of a window in hopes of pulling back some soups, a lighter and some Newports. Solitary confinement gave me a gift I could have gotten nowhere else: the opportunity to start looking for the sense behind the words.

I never found out who slid *The Black Poets* under my cell door. I did know the names of the five or six men who scratched their names into the wall of the cell where I slept. I knew the name of the white boy in the cell beside me, who'd make wine and slide cups to people for free. Across the hall from me was a cat who knew half of the people I grew up with, and when times were tough we'd pass a Black and Mild back and forth across the hall. Our lives weren't written about in most of the books I'd read. For a moment, reading Etheridge Knight, I began to figure that I could fish for the gray in the lives around me and write the life that I didn't see in books. Etheridge Knight weaved prison's hurt into poetry, and for the first time I wanted to write a poem that wasn't for women. A poem that was for the dudes around me, carrying time like the heaviest albatross around their necks.

The segregation cell was small and ragged. There was no screen in the window or plastic covering. Instead, I had a trash bag draped over the window's frame to keep rain and bugs from getting in. The paint peeling on the wall, the noise from the hallways, all that said prison. And all of that said it in a way I'd never been able to articulate, in a way I'd never really had hope of articulating in the short essays I'd started writing. I knew *The Black Poets* wasn't mine and that eventually I'd have to give it up, so I pulled out a folder and handwrote the poems I liked. I wrote out in longhand the poems by Sterling Brown, Hayden, Knight, Sanchez and poets whose names I no longer remember. I decided I was going to be a poet then, in that solitary cell. It sounds romantic now, but at the time it was a necessity. I started writing poems to Sonia Sanchez that I didn't expect anyone to read or care about. I wanted to capture a feeling that would make a one-man cell manageable, and sometimes now I crave for the feeling I had then. Doing something simply because I thought it would please me, so far down at the bottom of the totem pole that whatever anyone felt about me didn't matter anymore. So if I wanted to stay up all night, every night, reading whatever book I could get my hands on—from Reader's Digest abridged four books in one, to fantasy novels, to the poems that drove me to anger and yet left a settledness I hadn't known before—I was going to do it.

About that time I was writing to the ACLU for my man Roger. His case was bootleg, just like a rack of others I knew about. On paper it seemed treacherous, but it hung on a series of facts that could be disputed. The thing was, most of us didn't have the skills, the basic grammatical skills, to put together a letter that would make someone want to help. I'd gotten it into my head that the power in poetry that made me want to be something better could be woven into a letter that would convince someone to fight for a man's life when he couldn't. Roger had over sixty years for an attempted capital murder on the police in a situation where no gun ever went off. From the very first time he told me about his crime I kept thinking of him, and Terrence Johnson, and all those other faces that haunted me at night. All our stories rolling together until I understood that part of me would never leave the cells I slept in. I wrote the letter and the ACLU wrote back, told me that they didn't deal with cases like that. I took it as a fuck you, and for the months I was in the hole, poetry and time swirled in my head, knocking up against the words I was reading in the books and the crazed things we all said on the door at night. How else could I take it? I knew there were a dozen or so juveniles locked up at Southampton, and I knew that many of us had been sentenced to ten, twenty and even thirty years with slipshod legal representation, if that. But an organization like the ACLU didn't have time for people like us.

While all of this was happening, Red Onion State Prison opened. It was one of Virginia's first two super maximum security prisons. Twenty-four-hour-a-day lockdown. On some of the blocks you were only let out of the cell to take a shower. Its name was one of the great poetic coincidences of the Virginia Department of Corrections. A prison named after the one thing guaranteed to make any man cry if he got too close. If you read about it in the paper, you'd have read that the prison was for the wildest criminals. The COs there carried shot-guns and actually shot people. Every other week someone in the hole had a different story they'd read in a kite. *Kites* were letters in prison slang, a beautiful way of imagining something you wrote being able to fly as freely in the air as the cartoon figures you let ride the wind as you held on with a piece of string. People flew us *kites* that said so-and-so got shot, lost his eye. That said all the showers were open, fac-ing the booth and the block, so there was no privacy. Or this dude got beat down by a bunch of hillbillies 'cause he wouldn't strip. I started getting the stories firsthand when Roger got there.

The day after Roger left for the Onion, a counselor came and told me that my security level had changed to six and that I was being trans-ferred there as well. Every year they did a review of your security level and decided if you were to get put in for a transfer or remain where you were. If you had a serious charge, like my assault, they'd review your file early. The charge had pushed me to over sixty or so points, and that meant there was a bed with my name on it in those mountains.

Leaving Southampton troubled me. Nothing I'd heard about Red

Onion was good. I'd been in the hole for nearly six months and over that time I'd read a book just about every night, staying up from dinner till breakfast reading. All of that changed when the counselor said I'd be moving. I still read, but now the cloud of transfer was over my head. On a Sunday afternoon, not even a week after the counselor came by and said his piece, the COs were asking me to pass all of my property through the tiny slot in the door. In seconds there was nothing left on the floor. And by that night, the cell was bare and pitch black. The only thing in it that could be moved was a roll of toilet paper, a mattress thinner than the soles of my boots and me.

I stood at the bars and stared at the darkness, lost in thought. That night, after midnight, the halls vibrated with conversations. In a few hours the van would be there to get me. Someone yelled out, "Shy, you ready? That muthafuckin bus coming regardless, get your ass up. Ain't no sleep tonight."

They couldn't see me already on the door. I yelled out, "I'm here." I wasn't though, I was riding on the tendrils of smoke that kicked off the Black and Mild in my hand. I mostly didn't smoke, but stress is stress. Everybody deals with it differently, and that night I was dealing with it by trying to read my future through the smoke running away from gravity. Across from me was Lil Train. He knew folks I knew. We shared packs of cookies when the money was low. Train and I had the same amount of time. Down the hall was Big Youngin. He'd been down for like twelve years and was from Suitland, too. I was down South and still right around the corner from where I grew up. Either we were finding the prisons or somebody was putting all the bullshit that led us to those cells in front of us.

I was strip-searched that day before leaving the cell, surprised by a CO who came to get me at two a.m.—transfers usually happened around six a.m. or later. The hall jumped with good-byes and fuck yous when I left. The place seemed dirtier then, and I wasn't sure if it was because I was leaving or because I never wanted to be there.

There were five of us being transferred and we were led to the front of the prison. By now it was Christmastime again, the third in a row that marked a move for me. First it was jail, then the receiving center and finally it was to a super max. We were shackled and cuffed, then led to the van. It was still blue-black outside.

PART III

We Never Know

In the street outside a school
what children learn
possesses them.

—Audre Lorde, "The Bees"

26

Fifteen Hours to a Super Max

Thirty minutes after leaving Southampton we pulled into the
Greensville Correctional Center parking lot, where only a collection of faded white buildings and barbed-wire fences were
visible. The place looked like an abandoned warehouse, yet I knew
there were people behind the walls. I couldn't imagine life there. A
prison bus with VDOC painted several times in bold black letters
on its side and a blue van waited for us. Five of us were split between
the van and the bus, which was a moving advertisement for the Virginia Department of Corrections. It might as well have said: We Got
Black Boys. That was the running theme of my experience. Not just
a generation of young dudes locked up, but a couple generations of
black men married to a life of count times and chow calls. I rode in
the van, a seat to myself, and was sleeping as soon as both vehicles
began the long trip to the Onion.

I woke up hog-tied, a blue box holding the cuffs around my
wrists in place and a chain-link belt around my waist leading to the

shackles at my feet. I'd gone to sleep the same way. Marked, like the rest of the men in the van with me. Nine black men. We were brothers, cousins, sons, fathers, nephews or grandfathers to people on the street who said our names in the hushed tones used to talk about bad news. I heard wild stories that day. Only me and another young kid, B., had come from Southampton. He had a bullshit assault charge, too, and had spent over a year in the hole. The rest of the men in the van were from Greensville. Two stood out. The tall, light-skinned brother in the front row was funny. He was thin and older. In his forties. Green Eyes to the men that bidded with him. Tone, the other brother, was his opposite, a young dude who looked like he swallowed the weight pile and sported enough tattoos on his arms, shoulders and neck for everyone in the van. His tattoos marked him as a Five Percenter. The old head had run his time up. I listened as he told the story again because someone asked. Somebody had been fucking with him and he was six months away from getting out.

Green Eyes said, "I could have let it go. They had me working in the kitchen and the muthafucka was pushing every day. I don't know. The day it jumped off, I wasn't thinking about flipping on him. I walked into the kitchen, though, and he was at his shit. Then I walked out like I'd forgotten something." He told us when he came back he had a banger with him, an ice pick that he slipped in the dude's stomach again and again. From what I gathered the fight was ten years ago and he told the story then changed the topic as if it was nothing. The next thing I knew he was making jokes about the other cat. "Tone, what you gonna do when those rednecks tell you to strip? You can't hide all them tattoos." For a minute everything he said was about race and how the rednecks on the mountain weren't trying to hear no black power shit.

Red Onion State Prison was in Pound, Virginia. Nothing but white folks out there, and we'd already heard stories of beatings. It was mining territory and since the mines had shut down prison was offering the greatest employment prospects. The jokes about the racism up there broke the tension but also said something. Like the story about the boy who refused to strip. One guy on the van had been at the Onion before and had just come down to Greensville to go to court. He told us they beat that boy down until he didn't have no clothes on and then carried his naked ass across the yard to the hole. Left him in there naked, too. It was all a reminder that some of these white COs had never seen black people before and would treat you like dirt in a minute.

After seven hours of driving we pulled up into an empty corner of the Marion Treatment Center, Virginia's only mental health prison. The COs stopped so we could use the Porta-Potty. A sergeant stood five feet away from the van with a shotgun in hand while we each walked in handcuffs and shackles to the bathroom. The stained yellow plastic of the Port-o-Potty smelled like the piss had been on the walls and toilet seats since the day I got locked up. There was no running water. Though we were shackled and cuffed, most of us managed to step in and out quickly. Once back in the van they gave us bag lunches. Even if there was a way to comfortably raise our hands to our mouths, why we'd want to eat after pissing with handcuffs and shackles on was beyond me. So I didn't.

We would spend fifteen hours on the road headed to Red Onion. Our bodies bumping around as we held our useless cuffed hands in prayer. Red Onion was in a county a flight away from anyone who loved me, and I didn't pretend I'd be getting a visit. Especially since I knew the prison I was going to didn't allow contact visits. There are no words to capture the craziness that ran through my head during that drive. And nothing at Southampton prepared me for Red Onion's intake process. The prison was on a mountain and several people claimed a graveyard was the first thing they saw riding up the curved road, but all I saw was dirt and rocks. Outside of the prison over a dozen officers equipped with stun guns, dogs and a video camera waited. They took us off the van one at a time, because it was their policy to have two officers escort any prisoner who was in handcuffs. I was fourth off the bus, my hair knotty and shooting all over the place. They led me to a room with a clear door and windows instead of walls. Half a dozen officers, including a woman with a video camera, stood before me. I saw the stun guns and the dog. Up until then I'd never seen a stun gun or video camera in prison, but somehow it failed to surprise me.

I have lived things I will not recover from. It wasn't that they told me to strip naked, that I stood before a group of white officers with nothing on and a video camera running. It wasn't even that they recorded it or that in the back of my mind I knew three or four of the hefty white boys with uniforms would storm in at my first hesitation. My bloodshot eyes registered nothing as I was strip-searched, when I squatted, coughed and lifted my feet to be checked. I had nothing but anger to throw at the indignity of opening my mouth and squatting as fifteen people stared at my nakedness with indifference and fascination. Red Onion forced me to consider how I'd handle the weight of a jail cell and the memory of the woman holding the camera and the grinning white faces who said, "Strip."

27

How to Make a Knife in Prison

ed Onion. A different planet with large clean cells and COs with shotguns. I walked straight from a dozen eyes on my naked body to a cell in the hole. The ninety days in segregation I'd gotten at Southampton followed me. I lost my days between the pages of Sonia Sanchez's *Under a Soprano Sky*, scrawling poems on the back of request forms and doing push-ups in sets of thirty. The air was so dry my lips cracked and bled. I couldn't buy lotion or ChapStick until I was off segregation, and that wasn't for two weeks. On Wednesdays we went to the yard for an hour for rec. It was winter, the mountain air another fist going upside my head. The rec yard was a large triangular space without a roof, and a CO held a shotgun over us as we walked in circles.

One afternoon on the yard I overheard a conversation about how to make a knife with what they gave us. A knife, a speed, a shank—it was all the same thing. A little piece of metal or plastic carved into a point sharp enough to pierce flesh. "There's metal all over the place. Metal, and a little water on the floor. Sharpen at an angle." I took notes in my head, walking in a circle just behind them as if I was lost in my own world. Minutes later I was listening to advice on getting transferred to Marion. Someone wanted a way inside the cuckoo's nest, where there wasn't a need for knives—just Thorazine. Isaac told a young boy, "Just rub shit all over your body. On your face, too. You be on the next bus up out of here."

When I walked into my cell for the first time I thought there would be serious problems, so I didn't unpack my property. My cell partner was Isaac, the young dude telling the stories of shanks and madness. Within an hour I learned he had ninety years with no parole. He was twenty-six years old, walking around with crazy time like the rest of the young boys on the block. Once the parole board sent him a letter saying he'd made parole, and then they sent him a letter saying it was a mistake. Isaac was holding a clock with no hands. A Chicago native, something had gotten into his head that it was all right to pull a shotgun out on random people in the street demanding their money. He was a juvenile when he did it, but would carry the memory of the crime with him forever. I'd just turned eighteen when we met and he knew more about prison than I wanted to. He taught me what he knew: how to make a knife out of the plastic lockers, how to make a knife out of the metal intercom on the wall. How to sharpen the blade on the ground. For weeks he told me he would let me see his knife. Most of the time he didn't talk, but he would tell me about the knife as he sat on the bottom bunk reading *Gray's Anatomy*. I wondered who read *Gray's Anatomy* in prison, but he told me you could learn how to break people's arms and shit if you read it closely.

On the block, every kind of distrust was in the air. It felt like a prison. There were more strange faces than known faces. But Roger was there and after a few days we met on the yard and he let me known how things were. A lot of people getting played for weak,

fights breaking out and the COs shooting people. The place wasn't
Southampton. The small cliques all hung together a little tighter, and
a different kind of anger and frustration dominated. The block was a
collection of men who spent time in prisons all across Virginia. Some
had just gotten locked up and some had been locked up for decades.
There was no attempt to move you into a cell with someone you
were compatible with. You were just put in a cell. The very structure
of the place heightened tension. COs stood over us every second of
the day with shotguns. The showers faced the booth, and there were
no doors on the six single stalls that were the only showers on the
two-floor block. During rec or the moments leading up to chow,
men would be in the showers while other men could look over their
shoulders and watch the naked men bathe.

There were only two channels on the TV. Phone calls were close to
twenty dollars for fifteen minutes and there was no library. The time
we spent outside was limited and even then there was just one basketball court that few people played on since it was against the rules
to have tennis shoes. Red Onion was a prison full of men wearing
deck shoes and flip-flops. And there were no weights. People dealt
with it though. In the cell Isaac and I played tonk for push-ups. We
played rock, paper, scissors for push-ups. We reread the same books
again and again. I wrote poems. When we were in the block for rec,
I spent my hours learning to play bid whist. On any given day you'd
have four men posted up around one of the silver tables that dotted
the center of the block dealing out cards, twelve cards to a man and a
six-card kitty in the center of the table. Whist was like prison in that
the rules to each hand changed based on who controlled the bid. On
one hand low cards might be boss, on another spades and high cards.
It all depended on who won the bid. It was an old head's game, more
quick and subtle than spades. It was just like doing time. Every day I
walked around trying to figure out who controlled the bid, whether

violence was the trump of the day or the calm tone of backing down. And just like whist, if you didn't control the bid, you were often playing by someone else's rules.

At the Onion, everyone had a ridiculous amount of time or had been locked up for a ridiculous amount of time. When I got there, I looked at the hand I was dealing with and decided to be as low key as possible. I kept everything close to the vest. There was always a fight waiting to happen. One day we'd be in the cafeteria and a fight would break out, and if you didn't lie on the ground immediately, the COs would shoot at you, too. It was just the way they did business. Everyone was a target. A few people had lost eyes and everyone knew it. When I was transferred to Sussex 1 State Prison, I met a young black guy who'd lost an eye from one of the pellets they fired from those shotguns. He told me he was on the rec yard when a fight broke out and one of the rubber pellets ricocheted into his eye. How do you tell your mother that you lost an eye because the COs chose to shoot rubber pellets at two men fighting with only their hands as weapons, instead of just breaking it up? Especially given that half the COs on the Onion were six feet, two hundred pounds or better. Human rights violation claims were going out, but even if people were taking a look at what was going on nothing changed. Later I learned that the director of the Department of Corrections in Virginia, Ron Angelone, was quoted as saying, "What are they going to be rehabilitated for? To die gracefully in prison?" It's no wonder the shotgun blasts rang daily.

Red Onion was as segregated as the sixties, and since the COs thought we all had life, they treated us as if we were disposable. We were just black bodies surrounded by white officers. Not just the sergeants and lieutenants like at Southampton, but most of the unranked officers were white, too. There were one, maybe two black COs. Everyone else stared into our black faces as if we were foreign. At other prisons fights ended in handcuffs and time and the hole.

They even ended in blood, but unless there was a stabbing it was rarely something you couldn't walk away from. Those same fights could cost you an eye at the Onion. We provided that area with jobs and it gave us a beautiful mountainous landscape that we could barely see through our cell windows. Maybe it was the people who worked at the place who were racist and violent. They'd been told how violent we were before we came. They lived in the same world of handcuffs and count times that we did.

Prison blossomed contradictions. On one hand the violence of the shotguns and riot squads that came to break up fights was excessive; on the other hand I'd learned how to make a knife out of plastic. The reality was that the majority of inmates didn't have knives; they didn't have weapons of any kind and lived from day to day trying not to do their time. It was this saying: you do your time, don't let your time do you. And people would move day by day trying to find a way to occupy their minds with something that didn't drive them crazy. Even men who carried knives weren't always trying to instigate drama. I think about Isaac. One day he showed me his knife. It was an ice pick about as thick around as my thumb and it had a macramé handle. Isaac had been hiding a knife since the moment he'd arrived at the prison. We'd been on lockdown two or three times and had the cell turned upside down by guards who found nothing. The COs couldn't protect inmates when they couldn't figure out what was going on. Every time they showed up it was five minutes after someone got their head split open, never before. When Isaac pulled the knife out I realized that I had no idea who had what hidden where and you could never know all of what was going on. The person who stood before you talking about God might be the first one to rob you blind when your back was turned. Stories about prison are always filled with violence because the language of incarceration is violence. Men who were meek at home enter a cell and try to own it. And yet much of the violence existed because there were no other avenues to work off the energy men build up when they spend most of their waking hours in a cell. Isaac walked around with his ice pick and no one knew. Any moment he could have flipped out and started stabbing someone. He waited for something to jump off, and people who saw him walking around in circles thought he was crazy. But he wasn't—his mind was filled with the time he had to do, and to do it with integrity and sanity, for him, meant to be willing to stab a man for his friend. So he walked with his knife, and no one knew—and luckily, nothing happened.

HOLLOWED CHOICES

In 1968, Michael Herr wrote of the Vietnam War: "There were choices everywhere, but they were never choices that you could hope to make." He could have been talking about Red Onion. All around me there were choices, but they weren't the kind of choices that worked out in reality. People in a sane world would make those choices, but I lived in a world that had given up on sanity. That's why I learned to make a knife out of plastic and how to strap my body up with magazines. The prison had no school, nor were any of us given the opportunity to learn a trade. Our occupation was time. You stayed in your cell most of the day. And when you weren't in the cell you were always a moment away from lockdown.

On a Monday afternoon, two men from Richmond had been arguing while we were on lockdown. When the doors opened someone was punched in the face, then the scuffle began. I watched from my cell door as the older man tried to toss the young dude off the tier. That's when the COs began firing their shotguns from within the booth. The old man retreated to a cell, the young dude stood up. He cocked back his fingers as if his hand were a pistol. He aimed at the booth and took two shots. The block was silent, and then COs rushed up the steps and tackled the wiry young boy who had almost been thrown off the tier.

And then, after a few months, I was transferred. Out of the blue I was told to pack up my stuff. I felt different, as if I could do time anywhere because I'd done time there. I had the memories of it all. I wanted to say it was something other than violent, but there are stories that don't fit into these pages: The white boy who made a knife from the glass inside his five-inch TV. The morning the talkative brother with the goatee was knocked out on the way to the cafeteria. The man named Vanessa who had curled his dreadlocks like a woman's. It was time to leave. I didn't ask why or how, I just packed my bags and waited for the morning.

[28]

Sussex 1 State Prison

By eighteen, I'd been shuffled between a county jail, a prison intake center and three prisons. I'd been in isolation for thirty-five days and segregation for six months. I'd been at the prison deemed the warehouse for Virginia's most violent and dangerous criminals. And I'd learned to close my eyes at Red Onion to everything except moving from one day to the next. I read my books: I'd read Michael Harper's anthology *Every Shut Eye Ain't Asleep*, Sonia Sanchez's *Under a Soprano Sky*, Sun Tzu's *The Art of War*. I'd reread Frantz Fanon's *Black Skin, White Masks*. I read *The Winter of Our Discontent* and *The Catcher in the Rye*. I read books that I forgot fifteen minutes after reading them and wrote my poems as if they were exercise. I let my life be concentrated in the moments of one day moving into the next. In a poem of mine called "Reunion" I began to think about what it meant to be a black man in prison. I wrote, "I met my fathers in prison / they too a part of a scene / digging death." It wasn't like I'd met my father, but I'd met the men who represented my father's generation. I'd met the men who were absent all those years, and in that sense prison was the place where I'd met all my absent fathers—from uncles to grandfathers to great-grandfathers. I found out they congregated on the rec yards I walked. I learned to be silent around them, to mind my business. If someone pulled a knife on someone else, I turned my body toward the opposite direction and stepped off. When a dude got knocked out cold on the way to the cafeteria, I stepped over his body and enjoyed the waffles just like on every other day. I was learning what kindness meant when you didn't have anything. Kindness was Isaac teaching me how to make a knife and telling me what to be wary of. When the CO said, "Betts, pack your shit," I didn't relax. I knew I'd have to figure out how to bid at another place, likely just as dangerous and unforgiving.

Red Onion was a level six, a super max. The worst of the worst, as they called it. Sussex was a five. The COs there had guns, too, but the prison was closer to where black people lived. Waverly, Virginia. An hour away from Richmond and just two and a half away from D.C. It meant I could get visits again. It also meant most of the COs were black men and women who grew up in cities like the ones we'd grown up in. The prison was built on the same architectural principles as Red Onion. The blocks had forty-four cells, and most of the time they were filled to capacity. There was minimal contact between people in the different blocks and the place was liable to go on lockdown at any moment. In every cell there was an intercom and buzzer to signal the COs if you needed help. The intercom meant nothing though, not in a practical sense. When the doors closed it was just you and the man in there with you.

People always say crazy things when it comes to doing time. I'd hear sayings like, "Man, the time do itself. All you gotta do is show up and leave." Or I'd hear that there were only two days in prison, "the day you went in, and the day you came out." I felt every second that I was behind the walls and bars of the prisons that held me. I felt it in the names that I would go months and months without saying. Names I only think of now as I try to tell this story. By the time I got to Sussex, I was still young enough to be the youngest person in most blocks, but I'd been locked up long enough to have lost a sense of awe or shock at what was happening around me. I'd also realized that prison wasn't like they say in the papers. Sometimes it was worse, but sometimes what people said missed every one of those kind moments that kept me from losing that last bit of sense I had. I watched older people pull young folks under their wing for no other reason than they could, and there was always the rumor of someone helping someone else beat a case.

In 1999 I'd never met any man, black or white, over the age of forty or fifty something. I'd never had a real conversation with a black man. I met my father in prison for the first time at Sussex. He was my first cell partner, his hands were two shades darker than his face and they would break the morning's stillness as he buried the years, folded them into lines of print. His shadow on the wall was that of a man much younger than the sixty-two years you could see in every line on his face. An ink pen as fat as my thumb would pace the pages of one of the note tablets stacked on the cell's only table. His writing was a way of walking the cell, or the rec yard, which his body prevented him from doing. He wasn't my father in the regular sense of the word, but I could count the friends on my hand who grew up with their father, so he was a father just as much as anyone else in my life. He'd fold his body into itself like a church-worn fan, as he positioned his two-hundred-plus pounds onto the only bench. I wondered how he remained there, writing scores of pages to children he hadn't seen in a decade or better. His children, grandchildren and sisters all addressed in one letter.

Pop Jenkins. He stood akimbo, legs shoulder-width apart, body blocking the door, his eyes searching out who they were putting in his cell. First thing he asked me, "You smoke?" I didn't. Pop had spent time in the Korean and Vietnam wars, his life scarred by violence at home and abroad. I've never heard my grandfather's voice and I'd heard my father's voice once since I was four. Pop Jenkins filled that blank space with his memories. He told stories of the notorious prison on Spring Street called the Wall and the jungles across seas. He had outlandish stories that he dished out with a kind of authenticity that made the truth irrelevant. When he told me he chopped off a man's head once over a carton of Newports, I didn't blink. It wasn't that I believed everything, it's that I knew he'd been in prison longer than I'd been alive. Pop Jenkins had been down since '72, before my mother had seen her teenage years.

On the weekends he'd watch auto racing. The only black person I've ever known to watch auto racing and enjoy it. He became the backdrop to my first few months at Sussex. He was the one who calmed the eight young boys in the cafeteria ready to make something happen over a CO pushing his authority too far. We were all there together, the guards no different in some ways from any of us. CO Smith was as young as half of us and always had something to say. That day, Smith had been out front of the cafeteria when someone said something to him. I don't know what it was. Don't know if it matters. But after that, he was in the cafeteria acting like one of us did something to him. That day Smith bumped Yellow, a young dude from Portsmouth. Then he put on his gloves and stood behind him as he ate. Yellow tried to ignore him. When Yellow got up everybody at his table was ready to get up. But the thing none of us except Pop noticed was that the lady in the booth had her shotgun already aimed in our direction.

I say I met my father in Pop Jenkins's tired and bloodshot eyes because I had to sit and listen to him talk. And in listening I made the decision to respect this man, even though he'd spent all his good years in prison and didn't seem to care too much for the truth. He taught me, in his way, that the truth is often in the space outside of the story. It's different from history. History would say that he killed a man in the fall of '71, and that while in prison he killed someone else. All of that might have been true, but the story was in the way you had to walk around in the Wall. And how he could tell me about men burned alive in their cells. What he told me was backed up by the stories of the other old heads I'd met and would meet. Pop Jenkins taught me about being bruised, too. I watched him go to the medical department every day, three times a day, to get an insulin shot. He had diabetes, body dry and cracked by poor health care treatment and time. Staying in the cell with him was a lesson in what your body did to you if you didn't take care of it, and I began to work out harder. Three hundred push-ups a day.

Folks told me that before the years caught up with him, people called him Deuce. But when I met him folks just called him Pops. History had pulled a fast one on him and left him with nothing but a legacy of stories to pass on to young bloods—that's what he called me—who would listen. For a time it was good enough. It was the first time I'd come to a prison and didn't immediately feel this cloud of drama hanging over my head.

The days were smooth. Count times, chow times and rec. When I first arrived at Sussex they placed me in 1B—a transition block where everyone went when they first arrived on the compound. There I met the P-town boys. Yellow, Five Feet, Craig and the cat from New York, Keith, who was always with them. We were mostly pulled together by age. That and music.

Keith always had something new to listen to. He put me on to Mos Def and Talib Kweli's Black Star album. Their lyrics helped me get through some long hours in the cell. I could hear their lyrics playing out around me as I walked around the yard during rec and to and from the cafeteria. The lyrics let my mind drift to questions more complex than why we had fried eggs and farina for breakfast every morning. I read Toni Morrison's *The Bluest Eye* after listening to Black Star's song "Thieves of the Night." They took Morrison's lines: "And fantasy it was, for we were not strong, only aggressive; we were not free, merely licensed; we were not compassionate, we were polite; not good but well-behaved. We courted death in order to call ourselves brave, and hid like thieves from life" and turned it into something that talked to me and led me to Morrison. Music deepened my thinking. And the music was always hip-hop back then. I'd sit on the locker in my cell with my headphones on blasting music. I'd spent my life hiding in a way, posted up on corners and under the shadows the moon gave the night because I didn't see a place for myself in the world. There was no place for me in prison either, but there was nothing else to lose—and they say freedom is born when there is nothing left to lose.

I wasn't comfortable, but between the P-town boys and Pops I was cool where I was. Then they moved me. Transition time over. Time to head out into general population and fend for myself. I didn't think too much of it. Just packed my bags and dragged them up the steps to the block on the next floor.

Then, just as summertime approached again, I was in the hole. Again. June 4 this time. The prison had a policy to randomly search inmates as they left the dining hall. They wanted to make sure no sugar or other food was getting smuggled back to the building. In every block there was someone who could turn a bag of sugar and a bag of oranges into enough wine to get ten people twisted. It was standard procedure, but the searches were always cursory. The afternoon I caught my second assault charge I hadn't even planned on eating. I wasn't in the cell with Pop Jenkins anymore and my cell partner was a brother four or five years older than me from Norfolk.

Everyone called him Steel, and he wore his hair short with a circle of waves. For the past month I'd been writing his letters and letters for a couple of other folks. Personal letters where really all I did was piece together what they said to me with how the inside of a cell made you long for the last woman to say they love you. He asked me, "Shy Boogie, you going to dinner?" I hadn't been called Dwayne by anyone but family in a few years, and in a way I was settling into an adult identity distinct from the kid I was when I came into prison.

When I told him I wasn't going, he said, "Shy, they having fish." Somewhere along the way I'd stopped eating meat, part political and part a rebellion against the garbage food that I'd experienced at three prisons. Fish was a once-a-week thing, if that, so I went.

The rookie CO who searched me as I left the chow hall was three steps over the line. He grabbed me around the waist a little too tight then ran his hands over my crotch. Soon as he touched me I flung his hands off me, turned and threw my hands up as if I was going to hit him. It was pretty, the way I spun on my back foot and squared up with him. For a moment it was classic, then I realized that I'd be a damn fool if I put my hands on him and tried to step off. He started yelling assault and gesticulating. His finger pointed at me, and then I was on the ground. Then I was in a small holding cell unable to do anything but think for two hours.

29

Back in the Hole

S itting back in the small room in the dark, waiting for a CO to come get me and tell me I was on my way back to the Onion, was what they call rock bottom. For the past couple of years I'd been getting new update sheets every month or so, and on the update sheet would be my revised release date. Every time I'd gotten a new sheet my release date had been pushed back. I knew this second assault charge would push it back more.

Everything that happened over the next week was a formality that landed me back in the hole doing another ninety. In real life I knew it wasn't an assault, it wasn't close to an assault. But it was good enough to get me ninety days in the hole. My mother hadn't seen me in over a year, but learning I'd be in segregation always calmed some of her worries. This book is the story of my absence. Trips to the hole took me further away from my family, from my mother, but ironically it made her feel better about my safety.

On paper I was the same menace to society that the prosecuting attorney talked about. In reality I was a young kid who wasn't yet institutionalized enough to accept the treatment they handed out and expected us to take as normal. The pressure built from day to day; it came in the form of the laundry bags that came back full of dirty laundry, the stale food and the shotguns that were constantly poised over our heads, the violence that swirled around and made everything blue. Those conditions combined with the black nationalist rhetoric that still banged around inside my head, and I wanted to own small gestures of defiance. Not standing up for count, getting an extra tray 'cause I was hungry, throwing up a clothesline in my room because I thought having clean boxers was more important than a disobeying a direct order charge. Did those gestures add up to assault? That's another story.

Truth is I liked the hole. It was deprivation, but I could deal with it. The library at Sussex was the best I'd seen since I'd gotten arrested, and since my first stint in the hole I'd been buying my own books. So the hole, in some ways, was like a vacation. I'd bought a Walkman and some cassette tapes a while back and spent my days reading and listening to music. Make no mistake about it though, the hole meant being locked in a cell for twenty-four hours a day, often having nothing but your own voice to listen to. Yet it was a different kind of evil, and I'd long since figured out that I was the type who could deal with the isolation most of the time. Some nights I paced in the cell, staring at the wall and having conversations with myself about what I would be doing if I were at home or if I'd never gotten locked up, but for the most part I maintained. *Maintaining* was another word we used to describe a feeling I'd never had at home. It meant I wasn't ready to kill myself, but I was still in prison. How you doing, son? *Maintaining*, not broken down, but not running on all cylinders either.

I read more books back there than I can name. Toni Morrison,

Ntozake Shange, more Sonia Sanchez. I read Faulkner. I finally got around to buying John Edgar Wideman's books. Rereading what I'd read. Read some books for the first time. *Brothers and Keepers* was the way I tried to understand how my mom felt. By then I hadn't had a visit in a couple of years. Time was going by so fast and the excuse was always that I was in trouble. Me and my mom both used it. Hard to get a visit when I was a plane ride away doing time on a mountain next to a graveyard. Even harder when I'd been spending most of my time in solitary. Reading Wideman and how he dealt with his brother's life sentence made me deal easier with my family. I stopped blaming them when I didn't get letters. I started writing more whether I got responses or not. I knew that they didn't have the slightest idea what my life was like. I bought asha bandele's *The Prisoner's Wife*. It became the one book that I could introduce to anyone in prison and they'd love it. The hardest thing for a man in prison to do besides staying sane is to get a woman. Half the people I met wanted to know if I knew someone they could write and why wouldn't they? Prison was taking us farther and farther away from our minds and our families. No matter how we disguised it there was a lot of hurting going on and the world had divided us into predator and prey. The statistics and the institutional policies did the same thing. So when I read *The Prisoner's Wife*, I was touched. It was the combination of poetry, love and the woman that's down with you regardless that made it the ultimate fairy tale come true. It was a fairy tale though, and after doing a few years we all knew it. Once I got out of the hole, I put no less than fifteen people onto the book, and readers in prison aren't shy at saying you gave them a bad book to read.

Around the same time I worked in the block as a librarian. Each block had a small cache of books that they hired a couple of inmates to manage. A brother named Foots got it in his head to recommend somebody a Nora Roberts book. The thing was men were reading romance novels in prison for the same reason women pick them up at the grocery store, on a chase for some sex and excitement in the middle of long nights and empty days. The night the Nora Roberts book came back all you heard was cursing. "This muthafucka Foots got me reading about Ms. Daisy in Ireland. Talking 'bout, 'Read this joint, it's freaky as hell.'" It went on for a minute, and for a few days Foots was Morgan Freeman to anyone who heard what went down. But different books hit people differently, and the Nora Roberts flew off the shelf just like everything else. The secret was to know what someone wanted before they asked, and since I thought about that, I never got one complaint.

By the time I found out I wasn't getting transferred back to the Onion, I was straight. The system they used to calculate security points had changed. It might have been because of all the people that had been sent to the Onion without being true security threats, or it could have been because of the bad press the prison had gotten. Whatever the case, the rule change meant I didn't have to deal with the Onion again, only the hole. I didn't mind the hole, I could do the hole. I just didn't want to wake up on a bus driving me back to the Virginia Department of Corrections version of hell.

Every day in the hole a dozen different conversations filled the air. One afternoon I was at the door waiting for lunch and heard someone shout, "*Thirty-six Chambers* was the illest shit to come out of the nineties, son." I played the Wu album until the words on the front of the tape rubbed out from fast forwarding and rewinding. I jumped into the conversation talking about how Deck ripped the first verse on "Protect Ya Neck." That's how it was. A jumble of unknown voices breaking out of the cell doors into the only way most of us could touch home: conversations that sparked memories of days when cell doors didn't close all around us. One person would be talking and then five strangers would be on the door yelling back and forth for as long as the conversation could hold. Keith started it all, and I thought he was the same Keith from New York who had the cell above me in 1B. "What's up, Keith? How long you been back here?"

When he called out three months he had a question in his voice, a "who the fuck is you" tone. He didn't say it though; he wanted to know who was saying they knew him. In a minute he just asked me to come out for rec the next morning and holler at him.

Of course that next morning we both realized he wasn't who I thought he was. It didn't matter though. We had things in common: music and a chase for the knowledge that alluded us when we were free. In a world where you could hardly trust a soul, I kept running into people who were thorough, intelligent and trustworthy. Keith moved through prison in a blur of fists. In a time when people were running up their sentences and the courts were sending more and more young men into the prison system with crazy numbers, he was able to be quick to fight and manage not to add years to his sentence. At home it was rare that I knew someone who was a fighter and intelligent. Yet Keith held the two sides of himself up as badges of honor. Prison was different, the violence forced anyone with dignity to find a way to stand on his own, and the deprivation, the confinement made many of us want to be more. Prison was the first place I met men talking about revolution with the same ease they once talked about sticking someone up or bagging up ounces of weed or worse. Whatever the case, Keith became one of the few dudes I was real close with at Sussex.

One of the other cats was Joel. I met him on the door, too. I heard him telling someone that he'd been at Brunswick. Brandon had been at Brunswick since he left the receiving center. I started half listening once I heard that. Then he was talking about *White Ninja*, a book by Eric Van Lustbader. A book I wouldn't have expected anyone to be reading. Lustbader wrote books that read like kung fu movies and I'd been reading them since I'd run up on one by accident at the jail. Joel had read all of his books, and in the course of a few hours we talked about nothing but books. He was in the cell beside mine, so it was easier to talk to him. We could just yell back and forth through the vent, not even yell really because we were so close. He put me on to *Lord of the Rings* years before the movies were made. Meeting Keith and Joel changed the way I looked at time. Most of the people I'd known up until that point had numbers to do, and there wasn't much talk of going home. Both Keith and Joel were at the end of their bids, counting down the months before release.

After I met them, I started working as a houseman and my days flew by. Having the job meant that you were the dude who could help other inmates pass things back and forth. They stopped letting people smoke in the hole, but people had been locked up for years and smoking for years, which made tobacco a commodity. It created a black market where people who knew how to get the bags of 4 Aces and hide them could turn a profit. Keith had a hook-up with a CO for getting tobacco. It wasn't nothing big, a bag here and there. But when he went back up to population he was sending me tobacco. I was in the hole selling roll-ups for a stamp apiece. Three stamps got you three roll-ups. That made a five-dollar bag of tobacco worth about a hundred dollars. I didn't smoke so it didn't matter. Sometimes I sold the tobacco for extra trays, sometimes I sold it for money to buy books. I funded my education for four months with the money I got from one dude for tobacco. At night, I'd think about it and know it was wrong to have this dude's family sending me money. But I was nineteen years old and I wasn't ready to turn down what was essentially free money. I rationalized selling tobacco, told myself that I couldn't get the books to read and study without his money. There were no programs, no ways to further my education.

It was an older man who was sending me most of the money.

He'd been in segregation for five or six years. It depended on who you asked. James was his name. He swore he could two-piece a nigga to next week, that his hands were registered weapons. Prison had ruined him though. Left him fifty pounds lighter than he should be and paying more than what everybody knew a smoke was worth. And maybe it ruined part of me. The world wasn't black and white anymore. I was living in the gray area, exploiting the people who suffered like me because I could. I didn't even try to justify it; I was nineteen and had never pulled the trigger of a gun but had been to the worst prisons in the state of Virginia. None of the books I'd read meant anything when I went into those hearings trying to get out of the hole. From Southampton to Red Onion to Sussex 1, the hearings I'd been in were all formalities. A ten-minute hearing to find out I was always guilty, no matter the circumstances. The rookie told the hearing officer I didn't hit him, but that I took his hands off of me. That was how I assaulted him, by removing his hands from their place cupped around my balls. I walked out of the hearing and went to my cell to roll up cigarettes and sell them for a stamp apiece.

30

A Pile of Hair Around My Feet

efore I left the hole they passed a rule that said you couldn't have hair longer than two inches. My hair was at my shoulders, my locks growing longer by the week. There was a window in my cell. Small, just an open hand high and about an arm and a half across. I stared out the window during the daytime. When I learned about the rule I knew the Five Percenters were going to rebel. I knew the Muslims weren't going to cut their hair. These were the men, when it came down to it, who were ready to start a riot if pushed too far to the edge. Yeah, my time at Southampton had jaded me and I was suspect of the value of *doing the math*. But the hair issue was something to stand up for.

All of us cut our hair. I watched day by day as the ones who told me they'd do all their time in the hole before they cut their hair cut it clean off. The administration told us we'd get locked in the hole with no privileges if we didn't cut our hair. No books, no phone calls, no good times. Time was weighing on me. By that time my release date was early 2006. It wasn't nine years, it was more than nine years! For some reason they weren't counting my juvenile time and I was serving more time than I was sentenced to. I told myself that if brothers bucked, I was going to buck. I wasn't ready to lead anything, but I was going to stand up. But we all folded. Cutting my hair crushed me. They said that people could hide weapons in their hair. Weapons and drugs, other forms of contraband. I had contraband in my cell as I read and reread their notice. The contraband I had was brought to me by one of the COs. It wasn't smuggled in anyone's hair.

My mother saw my hair one time before I had to cut it. She and my grandmother came to see me, and because I was in the hole I had to see her through a glass. My hands were cuffed. My feet were shackled. As I walked into the visiting room I saw Pernell, one of my cell partners before this stint in the hole. His arm was in a cast.

"Man, they put this crazy dude in the cell with me. He hit me with an adapter while I slept. I knocked his ass out though, but broke my hand."

My mother and grandmother heard his story and wanted to know if I was safe. They wanted to know how I dealt with crazy people. My mom liked my hair, the hair I'd cut less than a month later, after my nineteenth birthday.

When I got out of the hole I was still a teenager. I'd spent twelve of the last eighteen months in different solitary cells where my mind threatened to unravel again and again. The system was burning all of us some kind of way, and right or wrong I was bidding the cards that were in my hands. But I was okay.

Joel was my next cellmate, and for the next few months we spent a long string of nights with our hands in socks, throwing punches at shower shoes. Things went on like that for a while, days just reading and talking shit in the pod. A lockdown here a lockdown there. People moved in and out of my cell as I watched bad habits bury men and better habits do them no good.

Jones, a cat from Houston who could really hoop, was in the cell with me for a few months. He was my man and had the smoothest drive to the basket I'd seen in my life. We'd be in the cell talking about ambition and what we wanted, and none of it seemed real with the years in front of us. Time was like dominoes we couldn't knock over. I couldn't understand how he was that nice with the ball and hoop but was locked up. On the block, four cells connected and if you cut on the light for one the light for all the cells came on. Every night when it was too dark to read by the sun's light, I turned the cell lights on. One night, while I was on the corner by the showers talking to some dudes, a kid named Danger ran into an old white man's cell and started stabbing him. Danger used a makeshift knife that probably didn't even hurt the man. The craziest part was that the CO saw it and didn't say a word. I walked away, forgetting what I saw with each step. After that the block went on lockdown, but just like every other day I had our lights on at six.

"Whoever that bitch-ass nigga is cutting the light on better cut that shit out." I heard the guy above me yelling through the vents. I didn't say anything. The next day, he came to my cell door talking real greasy, throwing around threats and making sure I could see that he was a good six feet four and two hundred and forty or so pounds. Jones stepped in front of me and told him he'd see him when we got off lock. I was lucky like that. I never had to find out how I'd handle drama because people put themselves on the line for me. Jones was going to stab this dude whose name we didn't know in the head. He paced our cell for a day thinking about just where to hit him. I tried to talk him out of it, but it was a done deal. And this is how any talks of the future and ambition were always being balanced on the edge of a knife blade. When we got off of lock the dude apologized. We'd been searched three times while on lock because the COs thought we had something to do with the stabbing. We didn't though, and they never found Jones's banger. The apology was a gift to everyone.

That's how the time went. Keith went home, becoming one of the first brothers I watched leave a prison cell knowing he wasn't going to medical, or the cafeteria, or the hole, but home. But there was always a rack of us left sharing cells and trying to make do. As I write this I realize that I'm reducing the days and days we spent together to a few moments of violence because it was the violence that changed our lives. It's the stories of violence that we went to sleep with and that changed the way we looked at the world. I had another cellmate, this one named William Stanley Jr. As I watched William make a bow and arrow from the scraps of a locker we had in the cell, I knew it wouldn't have mattered to me if he shot somebody in the stomach. Why should it have? Time was going to keep going regardless. What happened in prison wasn't new, and as people were getting beaten into comas around me, stabbed and worse, I couldn't let my mind get lost in their blood. I learned a language of violence and walked around like everyone else, as if the blood was the most natural thing in the world. William never did stab anyone or shoot anyone with the arrow he made. He was in for carjacking, too, which is really the stupidest crime you can commit. There's no money in it. Just glorified joyriding. People who sell drugs are trying to make money. It doesn't make it right, but that's the reality. People who rob people are trying to make money. There is no money in a carjacking, not unless you have someone to sell the car to, and out of all the people I met locked up for carjacking I never met one who sold the car. It made me think of the insanity of my crime. The hopelessness of it. William was the smartest dude I'd met in prison and he'd done the same thing.

After he got locked up he taught himself to repair electronic equipment. He made soldering irons and testing equipment out of scraps and paper. He figured out how to read schematics and wrote out the schematic layout for every piece of electronics sold in the state of Virginia. Once, he designed his own tape recorder, using the circuit boards of two Walkmans. Neither of the Walkmans he used had the ability to record. Still, by the time he was finished you could find two or three youngins huddled around the Koss headphones that served as a microphone making mix tapes, recording track after track of some of the dopest lyrics that no one will ever hear. But what did it matter? Jones was under the old law and couldn't figure out how to work the system so he stayed out of trouble. He couldn't figure out how to work it so he could make parole or end up doing his time at a minimum security prison.

On the morning of September 11, 2001, I was doing push-ups. Forty push-ups each set for ten sets. When the TV showed the first plane crashing into the Twin Tower, I was on my eighth set. My muscles were swollen and sweat dripped down my body. William hadn't awakened yet. And as the newscasters began to explain, to try to explain what was going, I kept doing push-ups. Then I stopped, I woke up William. In the days and weeks that followed, the prison was on lock, as was every prison in Virginia. I wondered what would happen if someone dropped a bomb on a prison, then I realized that no one would think to bomb a prison. We were the most expendable people in the United States and still, as soon as the first plane hit, the entire compound went on lock. We weren't allowed to make phone calls or take showers for a week. The officials didn't expect us to have family we wanted to check on. There was no sense that we would be patriotic, that our families might have been on airplanes that day or working in the Pentagon.

In a way, none of us were patriotic. True, many of us walked around talking about how we would quickly exchange our time for a term hunting down Saddam Hussein. But it was for the freedom not for the country. Somewhere along the line the penitentiary makes you feel more of a felon than an American. I remembered the stories of the old heads I'd known who'd gone to Vietnam. I remembered the poems of Yusef Komunyakaa and the fear I felt for my mother, who had reserve duty and often worked at the Pentagon. Truth is, the closest I've ever come to being claustrophobic was that morning, watching the planes crash into the buildings and not knowing what was going on. And then not to get any answers from the prison officials, just an announcement that the institution was on lockdown.

It made me feel so apart from the world. Around me men literally had thirty, forty and fifty years. The system really had no reason to feel we would be patriotic, except we were Americans, right? And if we didn't feel patriotic it was because somewhere we'd turned the American dream into a prison sentence. I wanted to wrap my mind around the idea that some of us were just bad, but I hadn't met many people in prison that I thought were evil. There were some people that I thought vicious in a way I would have never expected. There was Rufus, the old head who I learned used to knock people out and then rape them. Yet he never seemed vicious when I was passing him a cigarette or when I listened to him talk.

I began writing to a number of political prisoners around that time. I subscribed to a magazine called *Blu* that often had articles about political prisoners and included their addresses. I wanted to connect with somebody who had sacrificed their life for something besides a dollar, and there find some spirit of patriotism, a belief in the American ideal that I couldn't find among us who felt so easily dispensable. But I never did connect.

It was harsh though, because I'll always remember that I was doing push-ups when the first plane struck. I wasn't in college, I wasn't at home. I was in prison doing push-ups. Sometime in the future that's the story I will tell my son, how I was in prison when one of the greatest tragedies since slavery struck America. And not only could I do nothing about it, but I doubted, even if only for a moment, if the thing had anything to do with me and my cell.

31

Drinking Age

When I looked up again, I'd turned twenty-one and got one birthday card. It was handmade, a black man on the cover raising a black fist. From my folks Freddie and Joel in the block next to me. Freddie and I went back to the hole at Southampton. I hadn't seen him in years when one day he showed up with a black trash bag full of his property. The cards my family sent to me got there days later, maybe the next week. I was missing years. I'd turned seventeen, eighteen, nineteen, twenty and then twenty-one in prison with nothing to show for it. I'd spent over a year in the hole, read more books than I could count, and watched the hairs on my head begin to turn gray. One morning I noticed a gray eyelash, a gray groin hair. My spirit was anchored to faces that floated behind my eyes when I thought about what time meant: my mother crying, my little sisters seeing me for the first time in years in a visiting room.

Once, I'd argued with someone on a legal issue and decided to take a paralegal course. My mind was working in echoes. I remembered Terrence Johnson and told myself that I'd be the lawyer that he wasn't. It was about proving something at first. I asked my mom to help me pay for the course. In ten months I'd finished with straight A's. That's when I realized that it wasn't an official accredited course, which meant the classes weren't recognized by the body that certified paralegals. But it didn't matter. I'd learned some basics of law. How to research cases and write briefs. And while I was learning the prison system was shaking up. People were getting transferred every day.

I'd finally been out of trouble long enough to think I could get transferred and I was ready to leave. After a while, there's nothing to do but get vexed at prison's monotony. I was developing a stack of memories that all had to do with Sussex. People I knew who had died from cancer. The boy with AIDS who was waiting to die. Jones putting the sweetest crossover I'd seen since ninth grade on Steve. I could recall when my cousin was in the visiting room talking to me. A little youngin, Malcolm could have been but thirteen when I last saw him. Then, just as I was ready to get transferred, we were writing each other. He was locked up, certified as an adult for a murder that resulted from a robbery.

Malcolm got thirty-five years. I told myself he wasn't following the legacy I laid out, but I was the first person on my mom's side of the family to go to prison. For a while, some of my folks thought I was away at college. Or they just thought I'd disappeared. Or they thought I was the victim of some foul plot by the state. They thought someone snitched on me. It was a gumbo of rumors and maybe if there had been more truth Malcolm would have gone a different route. He was only fourteen when he got sentenced. I felt like my family was getting branded. Like there were certain families that did some things, like go to college and become doctors, lawyers, teachers, and then there was my family: not a college graduate in sight, not a father in sight. Pity is a terrible game to be playing from prison. But when I started to write Malcolm, that's the game we played. It was pity on paper, and clinging onto the only thing that had given us a rep, the few wild nights in the street, the insanity of what led us to prison.

I was twenty-one and was getting letters from my cousin and one of the childhood friends I hadn't talked to in years. Both of them were questioning my voice. Tommy, the cat I'd gone to high school with, the brother that was my right-hand man, right there when I lit the first blunt behind the Penn Station apartments. He told me he'd beat a manslaughter rap. That he'd beaten someone to death in a fight outside of a club. It was hard to hear. He'd beat a body, but the real thing was that the kid I remember making a joke out of someone offering him weed was deep in the streets. We'd changed without knowing how or when and we didn't have a language to talk about that. Instead we talked about words. How I said *cat* instead of *youngin* and sometimes I wrote out *son*. He thought I was trying to sound like I was from New York. Somewhere along the line our identities were lost in the slang we sung and the way we wore our clothes and even in prison I couldn't escape it.

And just as I read his letter I read my cousin's letter. Who told me I wasn't on that thug shit anymore. That I sounded soft. He was on his way to a quarter century in prison and he was telling me that I sounded soft. One of my closest friends from prison had a life sentence. He came into the system and was christened Juvenile, because he was only sixteen when he got locked up. Years before, when my lawyer was telling me I'd be certified, I thought I was different. I thought I was the only one suffering like that. But I wasn't. At every prison I met someone who lived under the same conditions.

Juvenile had been in the system for ten years when I met him and still carried the moniker that marked him as different from the majority of people who called a jail cell home. One night we were in the cell talking about parole. I'd get so irritated at the way people wanted change but weren't working for it. Somewhere along the way I'd forgotten how hurt will make you stop moving. I stood on the small bench that was by the even smaller window and looked out into the blackness as we talked. I was running down how he could make first parole when he stopped me. "You think it's that easy? Right now three percent or less of the people that go up for parole make it." What was in his eyes was the thing words don't capture. Some of us weren't going to go home, and if there is a chance that you won't go home, that you will never relax in a living room with your loved ones, the world is a different place. And I realized he was a good man who carved his life into a moment he couldn't escape from. That for months he'd been looking out for me and treating me like a brother with the world curved into a fist and pounding on his head.

I ask myself if it matters what he was locked up for, if society really cares about the blood that's spilled when black boys turn the streets they ran as a child into a battlefield, if anyone understands that we don't forget our victims. That the memory of the moment that locked us inside walls that cave our hearts in stays with us forever, and everyone we've ever hurt reminds us in our sleep. The truth is the names in this book represent real people, and whatever I say fails to open the cell doors that close behind them.

I wanted to explain some of that to Malcolm and Tommy. But I didn't. The reality of what prison was had been twisted by what played on TV, or what was on the news. Prison was a multitude of grays that I didn't describe because at the time I wanted to defend myself. I wanted to ask Malcolm what a thug sounded like, and to talk about the time and what it did to thugs and men alike. The truth was that I'd never been a thug, that it was a façade I wore for a while and got caught up wearing. But where did it come from? Some of us grew up in places that opened the realm of possibility to the insane and inane. To the things that we did at night that left victims and years haunting us.

While I was mulling this over, Juvenile was going about his days like the time wasn't a bomb ticking in his ear. In a way he had more hope than folks sentenced under the new law. The new law was passed in the mid-nineties when many states abolished parole and went to what they called truth in sentencing. It meant you were going to serve eighty-five percent of the time you were sentenced to, no matter how you behaved, no matter if you were sentenced to sixty years. At least he had a chance at parole. One afternoon on the rec yard I was talking with Righteous, a cat from Newport News, and some guy who had just come in. I'd just finished doing push-ups and pull-ups. Twenty sets of ten pull-ups. Two hundred in all, more than anyone would think was needed but just enough to make us think about time a little less. The new cat claimed he'd gone to Suitland high school. He knew the names of the dudes I'd run with, he knew their stories, too. More than that though, he had twenty-five years in prison and there wasn't much more that I could say to him. I was thinking about freedom and he was just starting a life that was going to be about prison more than anything else. We stood by the fence, behind which stood the building that housed the death row inmates. From the windows that stared at us the people on death row could watch us walk a rec yard that they would never touch because their life was reduced to cells and the kennel-like cages reserved for segregated inmates. Righteous had by chance spotted someone in the window he knew. For a few minutes, the two communicated through a makeshift mix of lip reading and sign language. When Righteous asked the man in the cell when he was going home, it was like a silence took over the entire weight pile. I stopped noticing the people running laps around the gravel. I couldn't hear the people still counting out reps. I watched the face behind the window. I watched him slowly mouth the words "I'm on death row." I can't explain the way Righteous's face dropped into a sense of loss that was so profound he started looking around for a way out. On one side of me was someone I'd gone to school with but couldn't remember to save my life, just starting a fresh twenty-five-year sentence, and on the other side was a row of windows filled with people on death row. There weren't enough pull-ups to make sense out of that, and there weren't enough pull-ups to explain why I hadn't described this feeling to Malcolm before he caught his case.

In the end it didn't matter. For weeks vans pulled up to Sussex 1 State Prison and dropped off the men who would walk around those halls for the next couple of years, until they, too, were transferred somewhere else. Among them were those who would take the jobs held by people leaving. Someone would be a houseman and clean showers and toilets for twenty cents an hour. Someone would be the block librarian. Some of them would be in the kitchen. I wouldn't though, not anymore. One of the vans that dropped them off picked me up and drove me to Augusta Correctional Center. I was twenty-one years old and approaching my last leg. A short-timer with less than three years to up off my back.

32

Names

J-Rock. Fats. Black. Catfish. Trigger. Absolut. Divine. Wise. Star. Born Star. Elevation. Donny. Chris. Juvenile. Gee. Kevin. Black. Malik. Doughboy. Azar. Bennett. Kareem. Slim. "Six-Nine." "Can't Get Right." Mustafa. Solar. Big Mike. Bilal. Born Star. Yusef. White Boy. Steve. Jimmy. Trigger. Blood. Twan. Pops Spratley. Pops Gray. Unique. Damien. Reds. Raquan. Kicks. Base. Twin. Justice. Freedom. Ray. Lil Wayne. A-Dog. LA. Pooh. Los. Scoobie. Charles. Double Barrel. Cat Daddy. Jamie Dog. Green. Chinaman. New York. Chicago. Lil D.C. Green Eyes. Snake. I-God. Keith. Tennessee. James. Snoop. Jose. Tran. Salman. Mike G. Roger. Snoop. Messiah. Doug. Frank. Roberto. Mike-Mike. Bishop. Base. Frog. Termite. Perrito. Venezuela. Kufi. Smoke. Columbia. Peru. Mexico. Papo. Pimp. Daquan. Slim. Blue-Black. Tony. Roanoke. Jake. Marquise.

Truth is I could list names forever and not mention all the people I met in prison. I can walk down the street and see their faces in strangers quicker than I can bring their names up. A name for every minute of at least one day and I could sift through the faces I watched walk in and out of the cell doors and rec yards of one prison. And I'm just thinking about the prisons I been to. Over a thousand faces a year, easy. Faces blurring into each other. Faces blurring into the walls.

33

Most of the Way Home

arrived at Augusta Correctional Center confident that I was
going to get out of prison. It wasn't a dream like it had been for
most of my sentence. It was something I could touch, taste and
listen to as sure as I was hearing the radio station WPGC for the first
time in years. Not having COs holding shotguns over me every day
switched up the reality I'd been living with for years. People went
home from Augusta. People walked around knowing they were
going home. It made me think harder about what I would do when I
finally did get out.

My first week there a black sergeant threatened me with the hole.
He told me, "Son, do not come in my cafeteria with your boots
untied or the shirt out of your pants." For three days I came to
the cafeteria—breakfast, lunch and dinner—with my boots untied
and my shirt out of my pants. And every day he said something.
I wasn't being rebellious as much as I didn't like him being petty.
After the third day he sent me to the J buildings to wait for him. The
J buildings were Augusta's administrative buildings, which housed

the counselors, the school and the law library. After meals he came and asked if I wanted to do my time in population or segregation. I started laughing and when I started laughing he started speaking straight with me. I told him I'd be cool. That I'd tuck my shirt in. It wasn't nothing really. They drew imaginary lines and we crossed them, at least I did, because I felt like if I didn't it was a step closer to institutionalization. And I couldn't see following every rule they set up for me, when there were still no programs for me, educational or vocational. I was staring at going home and hadn't received ten seconds of what I'd always heard was the rehabilitation prisoners were supposed to get in prison.

Soon after that I was called into health services. A psychologist sat in a chair across from me and asked me if I'd thought about committing suicide. Almost seven years into prison and they were asking me if I was okay. At Sussex a man was beaten to death in the cell above me. I was in the hole and screams of "he bodied him" rung out. I watched the older white man pushed down the walkway with a nurse pounding on his chest. I watched a kid get his head banged in with a lock in a sock. There were the stabbings. The rumors of rape. The pressure of being in solitary confinement. The trip to Red Onion. There were all the names of people I knew who had forty and fifty years in prison to do. I could have told him about this. I could have told him about the boy who tried to slice his ankle open. I could have asked him what did he think, did he think I should have been considering suicide? I didn't though. I asked him, "What kind of shit is this? I've been locked up for seven years and you bring me in here now?" He threw me out of his office.

For three years at Augusta I hit the weight pile every day. Sometimes twice a day. We called it the pit and went there to try to push the burden of years up off our bodies. I was reading August Wilson's *King Hedley II*. It could have been any book or any author; it could have been Walter Mosley or John Steinbeck. It could have been any-one who had a story that matched the force it took us to push two hundred and fifty pounds off our chests again and again. The time I spent at Sussex and Red Onion were like a razor cutting into the meat of my face. Once I got to Augusta all I could do was think back on it, stunned in a way. At Augusta we went outside every day. Walked to the weight pile rain, hail, sleet or snow.

You could say we all wanted to be John Henry, but we didn't. We weren't racing a steam engine, we were racing time. How many push-ups could I break my sentence down to, how many hours hang-ing from a pull-up bar and straining until my muscles kicked back in tight coils. The iron was half of my rehabilitation. And Augusta was the first place I'd had a chance to lift. To lift and to enter a free space that was more barbershop than anything else. Stories kicked back with the dirt and dust that came up with the dumbbells as they fell on the ground. The signifying about our pasts, about the future, the trash talk about how much weight a man could lift and who would do what when he got home that said more truth than lies.

The problem was the weight pile wasn't going to do anything for me but make me bigger. I wanted to be a poet and figured the best way to do that was to start publishing in the literary journals I'd been buying. *Callaloo, African-American Review, American Poetry Review, Crab Orchard*. I had a list of journals I wanted to publish in. I'd been working in the school as a GED tutor. It took me a few months, but getting the job was really nothing more than filling out an application and going to interview with the teacher at the school. There weren't enough qualified people who wanted to be tutors anyway, and before you could be considered for the job you had to be charge-free for a year or two, so the requirements knocked most people out. The teaching was natural to me and it was something that I had been doing informally for years, so working there was one of the first things I wanted to do given the chance. I shuffled my days between work and going to the law library to type up poems to send out to contests. It was against regulations to type anything personal on the law library typewriters though, so you had to be fast. And fast I wasn't. Instead of getting caught, I started thinking about how I could learn to type.

The teacher's name was Ms. Pale and she didn't do much of anything. The four or five tutors ran the classroom and taught the lessons. I was working with people I talked to every day who couldn't spell or do basic division. It was a struggle because the GED program was the ultimate studying to a test and often the students' skill levels just weren't high enough to pass. I worked every day, and after a while I began talking with Ms. Pale about typing. She gave me a book, and each day on my lunch break I started teaching myself to type. Soon I was kicking out forty words a minute. I started writing a letter to every poet and novelist I'd admired. If I read them I wrote to them. I didn't know what I was doing. I asked people for advice but I wondered if a professional writer would waste time writing to someone in prison. But a bigger problem was getting correct addresses. The poets and writers changed from university to university on a regular basis, and I often sent a letter somewhere the poet hadn't taught in years. That's probably why I never got any responses.

I kept writing even without responses to spite the people who told me no one cared. I read an article by Tony Hoagland in *American Poetry Review* on writing with anger. When I wrote Tony Hoagland I wasn't expecting a response. But he wrote me back and told me my poetry showed promise. Being in prison, I didn't expect to have the support of people I admired. And without that support I'm not sure what kind of rehabilitation can honestly take place. Writing was my major rehabilitative tool. My poems let me see the world in a way I hadn't before. Not simply a world of cause and effect, but of all the nuance that goes into surviving a life sentence. But writing was also utilitarian in a strange way. The discipline that it took to sit down day after day with the same piece of paper and pen and the same poem translated into lifting weights and it translated into studying. Tony Hoagland told me poetry saved his life, and I thought that had to be the case for me, too. When I'd gotten my first book of poems, *The Black Poets* by Dudley Randall, I was a seventeen-year-old kid in a solitary confinement cell wondering if he was going to survive prison. By the time Mr. Hoagland wrote me, I was a few years away from release and still standing.

I realized that there aren't many ways to thank people who help you from a distance. At one point in time or another I'd corresponded with a political prisoner, an older woman who lived on a commune in upstate New York, a writer whose work I admired but had never met, my lawyer, the teacher who helped me get my GED, a number of people I met while in prison and all of the women in my family. I'd gotten these letters and responded in kind, never really acknowledging that what was happening was a process of receiving love. There weren't many good mornings being passed around, there weren't many kind looks. So we all waited for the mail each afternoon and hoped to find a letter with a piece of the lives we couldn't touch there. In the letters, I found parts of my mom, my aunts, myself that I hadn't known existed. The worst part was that I found confirmation of my own absence. Just like those women have largely disappeared from between the pages of the book I write now, it is instead populated with stories of people they've never met and never will meet. Our crimes did that. Took a machete to the bonds that made us family and left nothing but ink drying on paper to try to piece things back together.

Almost every week I was getting rejection letters. Magazines informing me that my poems weren't of the quality they published. I started to expect them and my preoccupation with the letters dominated what was going on in the prison. I'd be in roofing class thinking about which magazines to try next. I knew the roofing class wasn't teaching me anything. This was what the system called vocational training and it offered to teach me just enough about roofing to qualify me for a helper's job. It wasn't even a trade really, just three weeks to learn how to use a hammer, but that's what the system wanted to see to prove you were interested in rehabilitating yourself. So I went there and swung the hammer and thought about *Obsidian* or *Poetry*.

One afternoon I got the letter I'd been waiting for. *Poet Lore*, a literary journal published out of the Washington, D.C., area accepted one of my poems. It was called "A Different Route," and I'd included the names of the streets I'd grown up on and the people I'd hung around with. E. Ethelbert Miller edited the journal with Jody Bolz. My poem appeared in the journal's one hundredth issue and I mailed copies to everyone in my family. I ran around the block with the letter in my hand telling people I had a poem accepted. In order for me to run around with the letter, showing people I knew who'd never read a poem in their life, I had to let go of every piece of anger I had for at least those moments the paper waved in my hand. And that was cool, because it's rare that we could let go of the anger. It was rare that we could forget for a moment that we were in prison and actually expect people to laugh and shout with us over our bits of success. The poem was about coming home and not being recognized by your family. It went:

A DIFFERENT ROUTE

Last night I
took a different route
home, drove my Buick
towards a street I ran
as a child, a street that
outlasted my wind
and held laughter and danger
like small lies. I turned
onto Swann Road, a payphone
that once shouted loose coins,
now dead on the right. Years older,
beside the payphone, stood
the Popeyes, still rooted behind
Lancaster Apts. On the left,
a row of ever changing stores.
Safeway long gone,
my first kiss surrounded by
the black of its dirty gray and
red delivery truck, a memory.
I drove, passing three rows of
apartments that housed my child-
hood, much has changed and still
I see myself shooting jumpers on a
crate suspended from the Old Safeway's
rear steps. None of us stayed. Not
Brandon, not Oatmeal, not Antwan . . .
all scattered, some in prison, others in
colleges or on other corners. This
night I looked for a clue, a reason

why so much was falling
apart and in the eyes of the few
children there, out on a Friday afternoon,
I realized how consumed with the moment
we were. I drove until my vision blurred,
until chasing an old memory placed
him there, speeding like nightfall
towards me in a stolen car, hands
twisting the wheel, struggling to straighten
the tail, unable to straighten about to . . .
and he vanished, left in '89
when it happened. His name another
forgotten detail. I took a different route
home last night, visited old parts of
myself. A lot has changed and I failed
to find in the eyes of others the thing
my wife, my children say has turned
to stone in my own.

The Color Line

Prison was the first place where I was around blacks and whites, Asians and Hispanics on a regular basis. It was also the first place where I actually talked to people from different cultures and ethnicities on a regular basis. It didn't happen as soon as the judge sentenced me. For the first few years I was so worried about my own survival that I just thought about myself. When you are doing time at maximum security and super maximum security prisons, the lines etched in your life are rigid. Those were the years I watched people get shipped to Texas and other states in inmate swaps, or when Sussex II State Prison was filled with Lorton inmates because Lorton was closing. Those were the years when I might wake up and hear on the news about civil rights violations at the place I laid my head every night. In those places, everyone kept things close to the vest, letting their behavior match the guns that guards held over us and the time that most of us held over our heads. Times when thirty-, forty- or fifty-year sentences were regular. By the time I got to Augusta, that had changed. It was still a maximum security prison, but there were people close to going home all around me.

At Augusta, the rec yard was open, and twice a day you'd see hundreds of inmates outside at one time, separated only by the fence that marked off the two rec yards. I'd see people going to the law library, to school, to see counselors. I'd been locked up going on seven years and it was the first time I'd seen that kind of movement since the short stretch I did in population at Southampton. On store days, you could watch inmates filing down from the store with food bursting out of green bags, or small groups of men standing outside the commissary waiting to pose for pictures where they peeled back their sleeves to show tattoos.

And even though there was always a danger under the calm, there was more interaction. And it was there, really, when I began to feel free enough to kick it with white folks. Had I spent my entire time at Sussex or Red Onion, I probably would have left prison with unconscious prejudices built into the way I walked into a room. Maybe. But whatever the case, Augusta gave me room to break down certain walls for myself.

Before Augusta, I could name, maybe, five white men whose names I knew. One of them made wine, one was my cellie and the other three would have been guards. After Augusta, I could name ten white men I knew. I didn't know them close, they might have been less than acquaintances, but they weren't just guards or people I knew in passing. They were people I dealt with in some kind of way. There was the white man in the cell with me for months who refused to bathe. He'd jump in the water and get out of the shower smelling worse than he did when he got in. Then there was Smith, who worked in the law library with me. I knew him, but there was a distance there: I could never figure out how an ex-marine got himself in prison without killing someone, and he could never figure out how I'd gotten myself in prison period. So, to a point, we couldn't trust each other enough to have a personal conversation. And then there was Jimmy. He wrote books, and I read a couple of them. Fantasy novels, three hundred pages of small print on loose-leaf paper. I could say he inspired me, but I couldn't really say he was a friend. The point is that on one hand I met all of these men at the first medium security prison I was transferred to, and that even then most of them were just faces to me, as I was probably just a face to them. Or that if they were more than faces to me, or I was more than a face to them, they were more backdrop for me. I didn't see them as confronting the same system I confronted in court. I'd look at them and always assume they'd had to do something heinous to get sent to prison, because it was all over the news and the grapevine that white folks were treated differently in courts. Maybe that's why I never really thought of any of the white men I met as friends. The world was becoming more diverse for me, but the ground that we all stood on wasn't becoming any more even.

But there was this guy Justin. He was my age, white. I'm sure his family always told him that he had no business in prison either. It was drugs that landed him in a cell. A night when whatever he was on not only changed the way he was thinking but had what he was doing adding up to more felonies than he could buy his way out of. He worked in the library, and whenever books first came out he'd let me read them early. He introduced me to the Red Hot Chili Peppers, to Nickelback and the Dave Matthews Band. One afternoon I told him he was the first white guy I'd talked to on a regular basis in my life. He looked at me and asked me if that shit was supposed to make him feel special. It wasn't. I'm not sure what it was supposed to make him do. I'm telling this story, but I'm not mentioning how we'd argue over whether *Harry Potter* was worth reading. I'm not telling how prison exposed him to a black world he had never seen and that every day everybody locked in one of those cells saw something they wish they hadn't seen, or heard something they wish they hadn't heard.

"Shahid, whatever you make it out to be it's still just prison. If they move me from here to some other place I still gotta worry about somebody trying to fuck me 'cause I'm one of the few young white boys around." I was telling him about all the letters I'd been writing to poets and how few folks had written me back, how actually at that time no one had written me back. He wanted me to know that he'd have to deal with the same things when he went home that I'd have to deal with. I didn't believe him, but I could believe that on a lot of levels, the fears and threats he had to deal with in prison were always going to be graver than mine simply because he was young and white.

I didn't think poetry would pay any bills, which is why I wanted to be like Ishmael Reed and write in every form. I'd decided to take a writing course that was offered through the mail. The course paired students with published poets and required that I write twelve essays of varying length. In a lot of ways the course was just as bootleg as the paralegal course I'd taken at Sussex. My instructor was a little-known writer, the program wasn't accredited anywhere and it offered no guarantees. Yet the course gave me a chance to sit in the library and type essays every day. The course gave me a person to send my stories about prison to and it gave me a chance to hone my skills. Most people in prison don't have access to courses like that. My moms saved my life by always scraping money together to help pay for classes that offered no immediate chance of meaning anything but another monthly bill. Still, as a part of the course I wrote an article about juvenile certification, teaching myself the history of the juvenile justice system in America as I did weeks of research in the library.

Augusta's library was one of the best I'd seen. Justin worked there. Like me, he should have been in a college classroom somewhere, and also like me, he spent most of his time reading. When I needed to do research for an article I was writing, I turned to Justin. The librarian there would order books for me from the area's public library. I learned through those books and the books that Justin found for me that juvenile certification was a relatively new practice. The juvenile system had been created because the adult system was found not to be safe or amenable to the rehabilitation of children. Yet there I was, sitting in the library researching the history that led to the changes in law that made what happened to me possible.

In the article I tried to present the complexity of the issue, but I knew a laundry list of kids who grew up in prison. And we had charges from robbery and carjacking to drug distribution. I couldn't understand why the state would send me to prison for nine years where I'd get no rehabilitation, no skill training, no education training, but enough violent images to last a generation. When the article was published by *AIM* magazine, I was excited. The minor publishing success had me thinking that I could make moves as a writer when I was free. And still, my practical side wanted to be a lawyer, if for no other reason than to do what people said couldn't be done. I'd been going to the law library for over a year by then and realized that I needed to apply some of what I learned if I expected to be ready for school. I worked my way into the job as law clerk and spent the next year there helping people prepare habeas corpus briefs.

The prison was filled with the fantasy that two weeks in a law library could get you free or that you could pay someone to work on your case and expect good results. I watched people who could hardly read put their trust and their little bit of money in the hands of a man who promised them freedom. And in my two years working there I watched one person help someone get home early, maybe two. Part of the reason I started working back there is because I wanted to work on my own case. Not my guilt or innocence, but the fact that the department of corrections wasn't counting the time

I spent at the juvenile detention center as a part of my sentence. That was seventy-two days I needed and wanted. After years of letter writing and getting responses back from the state that questioned my intelligence and told me I had no issue, I decided to go the route of the habeas corpus. The library taught me that this legal document was the most precious thing I'd encountered in democracy so far. It didn't matter that few people I knew actually got reduced sentences through the habeas process, or that anyone had their case over-turned. It's just that the habeas corpus, as inefficient as it is when you consider the ability of most to produce one, was the last piece of hope most people had. And because it happened after the appeal process was over, it often happened once the person could reflect on events in a way that he might not have been able to if he was being fed lies by a bad public defender.

I filed my habeas corpus and waited for the state to respond. They responded by giving me my seventy-two days and then tell-ing the court I had no case because I'd been credited with the time in question. That was fine with me; my next update sheet pushed my release date as close to 2004 as it would get. And a few months later I wrote a habeas for a man who lived in the block with me. The judge had ordered him to serve concurrent five-year sentences, but the Virginia Department of Corrections was reading the sentence as two consecutive five-year sentences. I charged him two packs of tuna fish, a box of Ritz crackers and three soups for the work. Not even five dollars and he got five years of his life back.

Most of us couldn't give time back, though. Every afternoon I was walking the yard with my man Train talking about what I'd do when I was home and what I'd do with the rest of my time there. We both had been writing poems and trading books back and forth. He was one of the few dudes I knew locked up who had been to college. People said anyone could make a mistake and that it would make the best of us better individuals. The people who say that have never stared at a judge facing a life sentence. Nothing I was doing in prison would make me a better person. I looked around me and didn't see people becoming better. The whole idea of better meant that they had to be some kind of evil before. I saw some evil around me, folks I just stayed away from because I couldn't see how me getting close to them would end up with anything except me doing five more years for stabbing someone. Train was carrying around a thirty-year sentence for some robberies. I wasn't no better than him. My bad day just wasn't as bad as his. My family wanted to believe that I'd come home and make something better of my life. I did, too. The only thing that had saved me for all the years were all the people I met who were good dudes and steered me in the direction I wanted to go in. There was nothing in the system that was guiding us. We were the adult version of *Lord of the Flies*, with the COs most of the time little more than the backdrops who witnessed the rage some folks couldn't handle.

[35]

Pronouncing the Word *Soledad*

Whatever was going on around me, I knew that my release was around the corner. It pushed me harder. An abrupt move had me on the other side of the prison, and it changed the makeup of the block. There were about twenty Hispanics in the block, but there was also my man Ant who was learning Spanish. He had a book from the library and sat down every day to learn a little bit. As he talked with the Spanish dudes around us, he caught on.

I'd been thinking about Spanish for years. All of the years studying French had amounted to nothing, and I figured with release so close I could either learn Spanish or not. After Ant moved into the cell with me, I knew I'd learn Spanish. I couldn't get around it. With his release only a few weeks or so away, I wanted to push myself to learn. I'd read a book about George Jackson years before called *Soledad Brothers*, and as time went on I'd learned the word meant *solitude* in Spanish. I also learned that it was the name of a prison in California. Once I began to study Spanish I wrote a long essay about how learning to speak another language allowed me to break out of *soledad*.

I studied Spanish for three hours every day by working through one of the textbooks I found in the library, writing every page in longhand, then doing the assignments and giving them to another inmate to grade. Each morning I'd wake up and study an hour before breakfast, then I'd study an hour at lunch and an hour before dinner. It became a habit, and it became a way for me to enter another world. Jorge was basically my tutor. He'd grown up speaking Spanish and had taken Spanish grammar classes in college. It took me a week to learn how to make my tongue form the shape it took to roll an *r*. Spanish made me humble. It let me into another world. I'd been meeting people from Latin America since I'd been locked up, and there was always a language barrier that kept me from connecting with them. I finally began to hear the difference in accents among the Hondurans, Mexicans, El Salvadorans and the other countries that were represented in the small block of a Virginia prison. My world before prison was black and white. My world for the first six or seven years in prison was drawn along racial lines. These lines were moving as I prepared to go home, and it dawned on me that prison was the most diverse place I'd ever been. The first place where I could talk to white folks, black folks and Hispanics without throwing on a façade. The walls around me were just as thick, but they weren't holding me in like they had been when I was a sixteen-year-old kid trying to find a shortcut to get home.

Every Admission Amounts to This

Before I turned twelve, my moms taught me everything I needed to know to survive prison. And if I did survive those nights in cells, it is because I remembered that she woke up mornings before five to get to work every day. That no matter how hard it was to pay the rent from one month to the next, she never once used my father's absence as an excuse, never once spoke a foul word about the man I'd only truly meet when a cell door closed with me inside it. My moms dreamed I'd do the things in this world she hadn't done, but never dreamed I'd find my way into a jail cell. There is someone, somewhere saying that I had much too much responsibility as a kid. That I was the poster child for latchkey kids all over, living in a small city with no after-school programs and just my own advice to get me through the afternoons. And all of that may be true, except around our apartment there were books everywhere. Novels and math books that worked their way off bookshelves and out of closets into my hands. From the moment I was born until the day handcuffs were first slipped onto my wrists, my mom's was the first voice I heard in the morning, the first voice I heard when I came home from school and the first voice sounding in my head when I started to turn the wrong corners. The person I most expected to make proud. In a second all that changed, and when it did there was nothing left but her silence. When my life became a derailed train I was left with the silence of my mother. It was never that she didn't talk to me, but that somewhere along the line a silence entered our lives. It was the place where explanations should have been, but there aren't good explanations for being on the wrong side of a cell door closing. This book is everything she doesn't know because of a wild moment in which I became someone else and almost ruined my life. This story tells how a son can scar everyone he's ever loved in the time it takes to walk to the convenience store and back.

I grew up believing that I'd be different. That I could duck the violence that was around me. I remember days when I ran from fights, my feet flying me past every neighborhood boy who wanted to see if I could go toe-to-toe with Lincoln, with Antonio—with whoever my mouth got me in trouble with on that particular day. My moms wasn't the type to walk me back outside and make me knuckle up, and she wasn't ashamed of thinking the world had to be more complex than a jab followed by a hook, that there had to be something more important in the world than how fast you could pump your fists. Somewhere along the line I stopped believing that the world was more than a combination of jabs and hooks, and right around that time the inside of a jail cell started calling my name.

I've always wondered why the books I read before I'd gotten locked up didn't save my life, especially since everyone I'd met in prison could see how writing and reading changed my vision of the world. There are no simple answers though. I had it in my mind that I could write a book that would show how I climbed out of the hole I'd dug myself into, but there is no blueprint. Before I committed my crime I thought I was different. I thought my robbery would not lead to death, and thought that it would not lead to a life of crime. And even after my arrest I thought I was different, thought my co-defendant and I were juveniles sacrificed by the courts, thought the courts certified few juveniles as adults, but prison taught me different. Each prison has a cast of men who once were juveniles among men. Some of these men adapted; prison perverted others, forced them to become other than they wanted to be; others made their own choices, learned to chew anger until it was digested or became violence; a few I met prospered in ruins. In eight years the most important thing I learned was that I am no different, that all manner of men call cells their home, and that the early fear was justified even if the demons I met paled in comparison to the ones I dreamed.

Maybe there is no real why, no one definitive answer to give people when they ask, "Why did you do it?" After eight years in prison answers didn't come any easier. The words that begin to say something useful about what leads a sixteen-year-old to pick up a gun for the first time and tap gently on someone's window before demanding his car don't excuse why I did it. The excuses have become unspeakable, and if anything the words fail now for lack of weight more than anything else. They fail for not being heavy enough to fall from my lips. I have seen things I will not recover from. And from those things I fashioned somewhat of a life. The day I left I carried the clothes on my back and a small box with some things I thought I couldn't leave there. A few letters, a book. Nothing much. To get out of the prison I walked down the long boulevard leading past the rec yard and the buildings that housed everyone. People knew I was leaving. They'd known for some time. It was the kind of moment you would see in a movie, me leaving, and just in my line of sight a boy who was a few years younger than me stood with his hands gripping the fence as he stared out toward the parking lot. It was a Thursday when I left. No visitors were coming. He was looking for what I'd looked for for years, a moment when he wasn't holding the fence but walking away from it. I could say someone yelled at me to take care of the babies. I could say three people told me not to let all those books I read go to waste. But what I heard when I looked at him was my mother's silence, and I hoped he could figure out the explanations I never found.

Epilogue

lmost every one of my moments outside of prison has been filled with me fighting to be defined by something other than prison. I learned to meet people and lean into conversations with an admission of guilt. "You know, I got locked up when I was younger." I thought I had to tell people, because not to tell them was to lie. I met my wife Terese in Karibu Books in Bowie, Maryland. It was a Monday and we were both students at Prince George's Community College. In a conversation with her months later I found myself leaning into my truth, "You know, at sixteen I got locked up." The confession always sounds like a joke at first. People rarely believe me the first time. My wife told me she never expected to be involved with someone who'd been to prison. Yet I've always wanted to be with someone like her, a person that judges me by who I am and not what I did. My life has been built into moments of hoping people will judge me by my character and not my past.

Two years after I was released from prison I sat in Howard University's office of admissions. The head of the Honors Academy,

Dr. Melinda Thompson, and five of my fellow students were with me. This was further away from prison than I'd expected to be. We were all, as a part of Prince George's Community College's Honors Academy, to receive full scholarships to Howard University. It was simply a matter of signing a sheet of paper. When it was my turn to sign the slip of paper, my right forearm weighing down on the brown table, I paused. The scholarship agreement had the dreaded question: have you ever been convicted of a felony? When I told the admissions officer that I had to answer yes, the scholarship became dust sifting through my hands. "Don't worry, it's just a formality. Once the committee meets we'll get back with you. Don't be concerned," the woman told me.

But I understood what it meant. I wasn't going to get away from my carjacking conviction just because I'd be graduating from community college with a 3.85 GPA, was president of my school's chapter of Phi Theta Kappa, editor of the literary journal and had been featured on the front cover of the *Washington Post* for YoungMen-Read, a book club I co-founded for young boys. My face fell back into a solitary cell as she told me not to worry, as she told me that they'd get back to me. They have never gotten back to me.

A few days later I received an e-mail from the *Atlantic* offering me the opportunity to apply to their prestigious internship program. The residue of my experience with Howard was still in the air. Before I applied, I told the people at the *Atlantic* that I was convicted of a felony when I was sixteen. I wanted them to cross me off their list if that was a problem. They didn't, and I ended up getting one of the intern positions. The other students were all attending prestigious schools like Yale, Harvard and NYU. I smiled when I told people I'd attended Prince George's Community College. I'd heard all the jokes about community college being the thirteenth grade, but I was proof that my education there prepared me to compete on the highest level. I was working in the Watergate building months after being rejected by Howard University and I thought that there might be a chance my prison sentence could disappear if I wanted it to. I thought that I could pretend it didn't happen. After the internship at the *Atlantic*, the University of Maryland awarded me a Transfer Academic Excellence Scholarship, a full-tuition scholarship. In both cases the scholarship wasn't despite my incarceration, but because the respective committees felt I was one of the best applicants.

Just as the summer ended I sat down with Mr. Westcott, one of the editors at the *Atlantic*. In my pocket I carried a picture of Terese, my fiancée, and my son, Micah, who was smiling in his stroller beside me. They were reminders of how far I'd truly come. Before I had a chance to speak, Mr. Westcott told me, "You know, I was carjacked in front of my home." I didn't know what to say. He knew about my crime and about the book I'd write. He never used the crime against me; he never brought it up at work even though we'd had a few conversations about the book. Every moment, even as I get further and further away from prison, I have to deal with what it means to have made someone a victim. I like to think that, as I sat at the table with Mr. Westcott and we talked about my book, he saw that I'd redeemed myself. Talking to him gave me a chance to realize that there are people who are willing to judge me by who I have become, and not by a moment of insanity.

Talking to him also reminded me of why I'd begun speaking for the Campaign for Youth Justice. I met Liz Ryan, the organization's president and CEO, while speaking about poetry and prison as a guest speaker in an American Studies class at the University of Maryland. In the months that followed I began speaking for the campaign on a regular basis, eventually becoming a national spokesperson for them. Being certified as an adult means that forever I will carry around the status of convicted felon. It is my shadow. As I've been given the opportunity to speak on panels at Georgetown University, Catholic University Law School, at the National Conference of Juvenile Judges and on panels at Congressional briefings, I've realized that it's not former prisoners who hope to leave behind the moniker of criminal. But people all over, those who have been victims or who know victims, want to hope that the people released from prison are ready to contribute to society. This book is a confession of what it was like to be in prison. It is about hoping that there can be more moments when people who have scarred themselves, their families and society can be given the space to redeem themselves. It is the story of the thirty minutes it took for me to shatter my life into the memory of one cell after another, and the cost of walking away from a bad idea a minute too late.

Acknowledgments

Thanks to God, who had plans for me that I didn't have for myself. I'm blessed to have a beautiful loving moms, who suffered more through all of this than I can ever know. Thank you, Moms. Even when times were the toughest you believed there would be something better for me. You were the first to forgive and the first to support. Without you I wouldn't have survived.

While I was writing this book, there were nights when I had to lock myself in a room for hours. Thanks to my wife for supporting me through those times. Through the times when I ignored her and our son to find a way to make words make sense on paper. Terese Marie Betts, you are amazing and without you and Micah this book wouldn't mean half as much as it does.

Thanks to my family. To my brother, Marcus, we came a long way. If I had to do it again, I wouldn't change a thing. To my uncles, Darren and Tom; to my aunts, Pandora, Violet (your spirit has always been indomitable, things will get better), Tricia, Bonnie and Linda. To my grandma—you wrote letters, you drove to see me, and you kept me a part of the family. Thanks to Grandma Betts, may she rest in peace. The visits, the letters, the silent support—that's how I made it out of prison with my sanity.

I learned that you don't make it out of prison alone. When you leave, there are all the memories of those you left behind, the names of people who made it and who didn't. For me, the list of names I carry and the memories attached to them is what pushes me to try to make something of everything I didn't lose behind barbed wire and cell doors. Thanks to all the old heads and young men who helped me make it through. I hope this book represents some of what it means to do a bid. Thanks to the brothers on the weight pile at Augusta, to the folks I ran mile after mile with at Coffee Wood. I saw the nicest ball players and some of the most intelligent men I may ever meet in prison. Thanks to Alice Holman and every GED instructor or prison librarian who ever gave me a job.

Special thanks to Tayari Jones. Without you this really wouldn't be a book. Your friendship and guidance made this possible. A few people saw early drafts of this. Thanks to E. Ethelbert Miller, Brother Yao, Erika Carruth, Randall Horton—your eyes helped me make sense of what wasn't making sense. Thanks to professors Valerie Jean and Howard Norman, who gave me his time and expertise. Thanks to my editors—Jeff Galas, who first believed in the possibility of this book, and Megan Newman, who helped me take a few hundred tattered pages and turn them into something I'm proud of. Thanks to Miriam Rich, Lindsay Gordon, and Beth Parker and everyone at Penguin who helped make this a living book. And to the best agent ever—Jane Dystel, my life changed after you called me.

There are names I didn't mention, names of men I met in cells when I had no sense and less hope. Names I won't write because I can't call them and ask if it's okay that I write their names in this book. These are the people who make this book mean something, and ultimately, I hope it tells part of their story.